FINDING INFORMATION ABOUT CHILDREN

FINDING INFORMATION ABOUT CHILDREN

YVONNE M. VISSING AND SHARON PEER

Nova Science Publishers, Inc.
Huntington, New York

Senior Editors: Susan Boriotti and Donna Dennis
Coordinating Editor: Tatiana Shohov
Office Manager: Annette Hellinger
Graphics: Wanda Serrano
Book Production: Matthew Kozlowski, Jonathan Rose and Jennifer Vogt
Circulation: Cathy DeGregory, Ave Maria Gonzalez, Ron Hedges and Andre Tillman

Library of Congress Cataloging-in-Publication Data

Vissing, Yvonne Marie.
Finding information about children: a guide to using computer and human resources / Yvonne M. Vissing and Sharon Peer
p. cm.
Includes bibliographical references and indexes.
ISBN 1-56072-974-0
1. Children—Research. 2. Child welfare—Information resources. 3. Child welfare—Computer network resources. I. Peer, Sharon. II. Title.

HQ767.85.V57
305.23'072—dc21

2001031271

Copyright © 2001 by Nova Science Publishers, Inc.
227 Main Street, Suite 100
Huntington, New York 11743
Tele. 631-424-6682 Fax 631-425-5933
e-mail: Novascience@earthlink.net
Web Site: http://www.nexusworld.com/nova

All rights reserved. No part of this book may be reproduced, stored in a retrieval system or transmitted in any form or by any means: electronic, electrostatic, magnetic, tape, mechanical photocopying, recording or otherwise without permission from the publishers.

The authors and publisher have taken care in preparation of this book, but make no expressed or implied warranty of any kind and assume no responsibility for any errors or omissions. No liability is assumed for incidental or consequential damages in connection with or arising out of information contained in this book.

This publication is designed to provide accurate and authoritative information with regard to the subject matter covered herein. It is sold with the clear understanding that the publisher is not engaged in rendering legal or any other professional services. If legal or any other expert assistance is required, the services of a competent person should be sought. FROM A DECLARATION OF PARTICIPANTS JOINTLY ADOPTED BY A COMMITTEE OF THE AMERICAN BAR ASSOCIATION AND A COMMITTEE OF PUBLISHERS.

Printed in the United States of America

Dedication

To Kiki, Chris, and Leah

and

To Jason

And to those who work to make a better life for children.

CONTENTS

BIOGRAPHICAL SKETCH	ix
CHAPTER 1: INTRODUCTION	1
CHAPTER 2: CONDUCTING RESEARCH ON CHILDREN	3
Select an Important Topic of Inquiry about Children	4
Refine the Topic	4
Review the Non-Electronic Literature Pertaining to Your Topic	6
Talk with the Experts	9
CHAPTER 3: USING ELECTRONIC RESOURCES	11
Library Electronic Resources	12
Search Engines	15
Refining the Electronic Search	18
CHAPTER 4: FEDERAL GOVERNMENT RESOURCES	25
Legislative Branch Resources	26
Executive Branch Resources	28
Government Directories	41
CHAPTER 5: CHILD POLICY	45
CHAPTER 6: LEGAL RESOURCES	59
CHAPTER 7: CHILD CARE RESOURCES	65
CHAPTER 8: EDUCATION RESOURCES	77

CHAPTER 9: CHILD HEALTH RESOURCES	87
CHAPTER 10: CHILD SAFETY RESOURCES	101
CHAPTER 11: PARENTING, ADOPTION AND FOSTER CARE RESOURCES	113
CHAPTER 12: MEDIA RESOURCES	121
CHAPTER 13: CAMPING ORGANIZATIONS	127
CHAPTER 14: RELIGIOUS ORGANIZATIONS	131
CHAPTER 15: SPECIAL INTEREST GROUP RESOURCES	135
CHAPTER 16: STATISTICAL RESOURCES	151
CHAPTER 17: FOUNDATIONS SPECIALIZING IN CHILDREN'S ISSUES	163
CHAPTER 18: PROFESSIONAL ORGANIZATIONS FOR CHILDREN	171
CHAPTER 19: CONCLUSIONS	187
INDEX	189

Biographical Sketch

Yvonne Vissing, PHD, is a Professor of Sociology at Salem State College in Salem, Massachusetts. She is a pediatric sociologist and researcher. She has researched and written extensively in the areas of children, families, and communities. Her first book was *Out of Sight, Out of Mind: Child and Family Homelessness in Small Town America,* her second book, *Childless Mothers: The Private Lives of Women Who Don't Have Kids*, will be published in 2000, and *Other People's Kids: Child Safety in Everyday Life* will be published in late 2000 or early 2001.

Sharon Peer has a Master's in Social Work from Salem State College in Salem, Massachusetts. She previously worked for the Salvation Army, and will be pursuing a career in gerontology. She was awarded a Graduate Research Assistantship, which facilitated her involvement in this project.

Chapter 1

INTRODUCTION

Living in an information society brings both blessings and curses when one attempts to conduct research on behalf of children. We may assume that if we just look in the right places we will find the information we need. But sometimes no data exists, while other times only poor or fragmented data is available. Yet often, at least some of the data we need does exist. The problem is finding it.

We found ourselves in just this predicament when we conducted research on children. As we attempted to find out everything we could about a particular topic, we found ourselves overwhelmed by both the amount of information that was available and the complexity in finding it. We also found that quantity of information did not necessarily equate quality. When conducting research, it is possible to spin your conceptual wheels for hours, days, and even years without finding what you want. It is important, both from an administrative and a child advocacy point of view that time, energy and resources not be wasted. People in positions of responsibility must remember that children depend on us to assist them. For many, time is of the essence. All children will grow older, many will be hurt in the meantime, and some, unfortunately, will die. There is no time to waste looking for information. We hope this guide will help you to help the children.

This guide is divided into chapters in which some special aspect of child research is the focus. For instance, one chapter deals exclusively with how to find United States government agency information about children. There are multiple institutes in Washington, each with multiple sub-units, and each which oversee multiple sources of valuable research information. Another chapter focuses exclusively on issues of child health, while another concerns itself with legal issues that pertain to children. There is an overview chapter for those who wish to know more about the intricacies of how to use the Internet to find information about children. Several different options are provided to assist the novice surfer with information about how to find desired information. The Internet will constantly be changing, but once an investigator has a good idea about the fundamentals of conducting child-oriented research, future modifications will be easier. The end of the book provides the reader with information on key child oriented professional organizations. Each of these organizations have unique and valuable information that investigators may want. The index is designed to be user-friendly, providing a quick guide to finding basic web sites that address certain child-oriented topics.

As you embark upon your research on child issues, we encourage you to do what children are often told as they learn to walk - if you fall down, get up and try again. If you do not succeed the first time, or the second, or even the third, if you continue to put forth effort and are creative in your approach, you will likely succeed. Good luck!

Special thanks are given to Salem State College for funding this project. In particular, thanks are given to Dr. Albert Hamilton, Dr. Marion Kilson, Dr. Laverna Saunders, Sociology Chairman Arthur Gould, Professor Kenneth MacIver, and Stephen Smith. Nancy Berndtson contributed considerably to the development of this book, both in site identification and editorial assistance.

Chapter 2

CONDUCTING RESEARCH ON CHILDREN

According to federal reports, reports by non-profit organizations such as the Children's Defense Fund, and reports from groups like the National Commission on Children, millions of children in the United States simultaneously live the most affluent and the most troubled lives than ever. Children and youth have more expendable income, have more material objects like TVs, stereos, computers, and designer clothes, yet they are more depressed, suicidal, substance abusing, and violent than ever. At the same time, millions of other children have no health insurance, are homeless, and live in poverty as they struggle to survive. Parent-child relationships are strained, schools try to provide a comprehensive education to all with needs that are increasing as resources are strained.

The future of American society rests on the shoulders of today's children and youth. Researchers and program developers need good quality information in order to accomplish the task of helping to assure that the shoulders of the youth are strong and healthy and able to be a firm foundation for tomorrow. But where do they find the information they need? This is the challenge for researchers in the area of children's issues.

Being a good researcher about children is like being an artist or a musician - the more you practice and know, the better the work you create. To become proficient and to make any particular work complete, it will take more time and effort than perhaps you had anticipated. However, the basic guide rules on conducting research about children are clear-cut. The rules are, briefly:

SELECT AN IMPORTANT TOPIC OF INQUIRY ABOUT CHILDREN

There are millions of potential issues pertaining to infants, children, adolescents and teens, but some issues are more important than others. In selecting the topic, be clear on why it is important and what you want to accomplish by selecting it.

REFINE THE TOPIC

Most of the time we begin our research by selecting a broad-based issue and learn quickly that we need to be more focused on exactly what we want to find out. For instance, let's say you are interested in child safety at school. This is an important topic, to be sure. But exactly what are you interested in researching? Could it be:

- why students are violent
- profiles of potentially violent students for easier identification in order to prevent serious violence
- how toys and media influence student behaviors at school
- number and types of weapons students bring to school
- numbers of deaths and injuries occurring at school
- policies and practices schools use to create safe environments
- availability and use of counseling services for troubled students
- peer support networks
- relationships that exist between schools and police
- curriculums that encourage peace and discourage violence
- after-school recreation and educational alternatives for youth
- parent education and communication programs that could prevent violence
- procedures designed to be used in case of emergency at school

The list of topics is endless! The specificity of the topic leads one to a more refined search for relevant information. There is so much information available that it is easy to waste time, resources and energy by being ill focused.

There are many things to think about when planning your investigation. What exactly do you want to find? Where would be the most logical places to find the information you need? How can you tell if the information you have found is of good quality? Who are the expert people and organizations that would be good contacts? Do you want governmental resources, or do you want information from profit or not-for-profit organizations? Do you want macro, or large scale information (such as health care policies for children in the USA) or do you want specific, micro information (such as the health care agency overseeing child Medicaid in your city). Ultimately, what will you do with the information after you get it? Anticipating what end-product you want will help to keep you focused!

The best way to refine and understand the topic is to identify and read key pieces of literature. This means that you have to do a thorough investigation of the important literature and studies. However, when a novice is beginning the research project, one may not know where to look for the good literature or who the experts are. There are three major resources most researchers use: the electronic world, non-electronic written resources, and interpersonal resources. Think of these three resources being different spokes of the same tire - each spoke links you to the central topic, as well as to the outer edges of it. Each spoke helps create the structural integrity of the tire; each one is important, and each one has interconnections to the other. It doesn't really matter which one you start with - you can begin by talking with experts in the field, or by thumbing through written material, or by searching information via electronic mediums. Each should lead naturally to the other resources, thereby allowing you the full field of available information on the topic. Using just one form of information is often insufficient - while the computer can provide you with extensive information about many child-related topics, researchers often fail in their task by thinking that what is found on the web by entering in certain keywords is all there is. Wrong! The electronic world links the researcher to the literary, organizational and interpersonal worlds - without them, there would be no need for the web.

The electronic system of surfing will not provide all the information that a person may desire on any given topic. It is important to remember that not all information is yet on the Internet, and some relevant-to-you-information may never be. Remember the old saw, "Information is Power." Sometimes people have information that they do not want to be readily available to the masses; other times people find it too costly, too time consuming, or too complex to make it available. And other times, people have internal documents or have gained important insight and expertise which may not be readily available to others. By rolling up your sleeves and digging into the information network, you will likely find what you are looking for.

REVIEW THE NON-ELECTRONIC LITERATURE PERTAINING TO YOUR TOPIC

It is surprising how often child researchers today forget to use the non-electronic, basic resources that investigators have used over the years. Go to the library and head for the periodical room. There are both magazines and peer reviewed scholarly journals. When you walk through the stacks of publications, look at which ones pertain to children or the topic of your interest. Flip through them to identify how many of what types of articles are available. There you will find magazines such as *American Baby, Child, Family Digest, Healthy Kids*, and *Parenting Magazine*. You may find the journals of *Adolescence, Child and Youth Care Quarterly, Child Welfare, Child Development, Children and Youth Services Review*, and *Journal of Children in Contemporary Society*. Merely by flipping through the table of contents and selected articles that catch your eye, you will learn a great deal about what is published, what is deemed important, and what is not.

For the most accurate research, seek out the peer reviewed publications. To be peer-reviewed means that the work had to be critiqued by three outsider reviewers who made sure the work was good and met rigorous scientific criteria before it was allowed to be in print. They made the author change or revise any incorrect information. Peer-reviewed articles, as a result, are usually reliable work on which you can trust. It is often more difficult to determine if material is peer-reviewed when you are scanning information on the Internet. The major problem with peer-reviewed journal articles is that it probably takes a year from the time the article is written until it is in print. Magazines, and certainly newspapers, contain more recent contemporary information. So if you are interested in how many gun attacks by students there have been at schools over the past year, you may actually be better off reviewing newspaper articles in major cities instead of focusing entirely on journal articles or books.

Assume you have picked a topic that is of long-standing concern, such as the psychological impact of physical abuse on children. Go to the library periodical room shelves and pull off volumes of the journals you think may have articles that pertain to your topic, such as the *International Journal of Child Abuse and Neglect*, and thumb through the tables of contents. I may do this for ten previous years. Some articles will inevitably catch my eye and I will scan them. When I find an article or book that triggers my attention, I look at it in detail and then turn to its bibliography. Bibliographies can be an extremely valuable way of quickly locating relevant information. Your colleagues may have already done a great deal of your work for you by putting together comprehensive lists of resources. Annotated bibliographies are another source of information that can help you hone in on exactly the written materials you may need. For instance, the National Coalition for the Homeless compiled an annotated bibliography of all the articles written about homelessness. It is indexed and provided me with volumes of relevant information in a quick and easy fashion when I wrote my book about homeless children. The National Institute of Child Abuse and Neglect has a CD with bibliographic resources of major child abuse publications over the last several decades. Whenever you can access bibliographies, your work is cut in half. Similarly, looking at current and past Books-In-Print can provide you with a wealth of information. Typically by the time research is conducted and a book is in print, a considerable amount of time has elapsed. However, a good book can contain a wealth of conceptual and bibliographic reference that could be of use to you. It is important to realize that books, by their publication nature, will always be dated. This may, or may not, matter to you, depending on what you are using and why you are using it.

Newspapers and magazines provide the investigator with great current events information. However, the limitations of newspaper, news magazines, and other popular press publications are that they are not necessarily written by objective scholars. There is no peer-reviewed process prior to publication, the way that peer reviewed journals demand. Newspapers make their money by accurate reporting, but sometimes this means sensationalizing a story. Time is of the essence in the current events publication world, and being the first to get the story out is important to them. This means that sometimes errors can be made in reporting.

Therefore, caveat emptor is warranted - let the reader beware. Some of the contemporary information is useful, and others are misleading or wrong.

When popular publications review scholarly research, they do so in summaries. Usually these are written by people who are not expert in the field, who could make interpretation errors, or who have biased views in reporting what they have learned. When newspapers or popular press articles reference other people's studies, this means that you should not take the newspaper writer's word for what was in the document - rather, use their citation as notice that an interesting piece of research exists helps you to track down the original article for a closer look.

Another valuable source of information are official reports. Many of these have been written by government sources, such as U.S. House's Select Committee on Children Youth, and Families Report on Children's Well Being or the Department of Education's, "Serving Homeless Children". These reports may be summarized in various places, but the entire document may only be available by either going to the Government Documents section of the library, or sending off for it. Foundations and private groups also write reports, such as the Grant Foundation's "The Forgotten Half: Pathways for Success for America's Youth" or "Beyond Rhetoric" by the National Commission on Children.

Through these types of literary research, you can quickly ascertain trends and information that may not be easily obtainable by typing in keywords into the computer library search engine. Computerized searches assume that you already have identified the bulk of information you want. When you are first getting into a research project, it may be necessary to cast a broader net in order to understand the full picture of the nature of the phenomenon you wish to study. Only by looking broadly can you then narrow your focus to ask specific questions. Thumbing through documents about your general topic makes it possible to refine your own thought processes. Also, one may learn when going through the literature that the big question you had has already been answered by others. It may also be that in scanning documents you will realize that you are really more interested in a related, but separate, project than the one you originally pursued.

TALK WITH THE EXPERTS

Research is usually best when it is not a solitary enterprise. It is important to talk with people who are experts in the topic you are investigating. Call them on the phone, e-mail them, talk to their assistants, or write to them to pose your questions. Experts can often help you cut to the chase - they can hear what your concerns are, and since they have likely already spent a great deal of time thinking through similar issues, they can advise you on how best to proceed with your work. They can give you both conceptual insights and resource information that you may find difficult getting elsewhere. Experts can also give you the inside scoop on which documents are credible and which are not. They also know about funding opportunities, innovative programs, and other information that one cannot obtain with a click of a mouse.

For instance, this handbook was inspired from a conversation I had with the research director of a major child advocacy organization. I phoned him in order to make sure I was utilizing a comprehensive data base of information for one of my research projects. He indicated that most people in the child research field had a core knowledge of where to go, but few people knew had a comprehensive list of resources that existed. He nonchalantly suggested, "Why don't you make one?" It was such a good idea that we did! We never dreamed that from a simple conversation that this handbook would result.

When you contact experts, you are well advised to be brief and to-the-point. They are busy people and you have no right to intrude upon their work by processing all your thoughts with them. You may be lucky and find experts willing to talk with you at length about your work and share resources. Others typically charge for consultation and will not be receptive to lengthy discussion - especially if you are ill focused. However, most child researchers will understand that you are trying to help this vulnerable population and they will give you at least a small bit of good advice for free.

While the paper resources and personal contacts will be extremely valuable, every child oriented researcher today will find it essential to access the volumes of data that exist in electronic form.

Chapter 3

USING ELECTRONIC RESOURCES

Some researchers are adept at using different search engines and library data bases in order to find information about children. Others, however, are not. This chapter is written with the relatively inexperienced computer investigator in mind, since many people who want to help children are so busy with administrative or action tasks that they have been unable to get the time or training necessary to becoming proficient accessing information on the web. Researchers who are more experienced using electronic resources may wish to only scan this chapter and move on to the following chapters, which describe computer web sites on specific types of information about children. Novice electronic media investigators, however, may find this chapter to be particularly useful.

The world of electronic research can provide you with a wealth of information about infants, children, adolescents, teens and child-centered issues, but you still have the task of finding the material and deciding whether it is of good quality or not. This is where expertise and practice become critically important. Initially, you may feel bruised and frustrated because you cannot find information on the net as easily or quickly as you'd like. But remember, you should expect to fall when you are learning to walk, and you should expect to walk before you can run. Once you've mastered the basic skills, you should be able to fly to the right locations and identify the best sources of information.

Looking for child-centered electronic library resources or web sites created by a particular child-focused organization requires you use search engines and communicate in the language that the search engine understands. One day, it will be easy to ask for certain information and be able to find it with a keystroke. Until that day, however, we still need keys to unlock the information contained in the Internet.

All too often, people go on a fishing expedition on the web for information, pulling up anything that looks remotely interesting. This is particularly the case when you are beginning investigation on a topic and are not quite sure where it will lead. For instance, after several months of investigation for a study we conducted on child safety, we found ourselves sitting amidst a mountain of print-out off the web. All of it was interesting - otherwise we wouldn't have bothered to copy it - but there was simply too much of a good thing. First of all, even though we thought our topic was narrow, we should have narrowed it even more. Secondly, we would have been better off to have used the edit command and moved web information into sub files on our word processor, such as 'daycare safety', 'recreation safety', or 'school safety'. This would have created neat files that were ready to edit, instead of now having to re-read what we thought was important and enter that information into the computer. Our project could have been done a year earlier if we had done this simple task. As the world of electronic research advances, we have to use new techniques for data collection that will make our products better and our time lines faster.

There are two primary ways a child researcher can use electronic resources. One is to use library data bases to obtain material from journals and other literary sources, and the other is to surf the net, using various search engines in order to find organizational and other information about children's issues.

LIBRARY ELECTRONIC RESOURCES

Today most libraries have computerized systems that will help you locate books, periodicals, magazines, and other information that pertain to child-oriented research. Common electronic library resources include the Library Catalogue, which provides locations of books and journals in the library and those with whom there is an established exchange program. Their systems will tell you if the material is available at the library and where it is located. If the material is not available, the electronic system will give you a sense of if and when it will be available at your library, or where else you may want to go to obtain it. For instance, your library may not have a particular book or journal you want, but an affiliate library does. You can request that your library obtain the needed material through its inter-library loan process.

Libraries have access to data bases which include key articles and publications in particular areas. In the 'old days', libraries would buy a particular data base, such as ERIC, which was one of the first data bases available. ERIC contains information about a host of topics related to the education of children. They may have also purchased MEDLINE, which contained professional material about a host of medical conditions and articles from the major medical journals. Over time, hundreds of topic-specific data bases have emerged. Some of the data bases that are of particular interest for child-focused investigators include:

Education: ERIC, EDUCATION ABSTRACTS
Legal: WESTLAW
Medicine: MEDLINE, HEALTH SOURCE PLUS, HEALTH REFERENCE CENTER, CINAHL (Nursing), EMBASE (International health and pharmaceutical information)
Population/demography: POPLINE, POPULATION INDEX, CENSUS TRACT DATA
Psychological: PSYCINFO, MENTAL HEALTH ABSTRACTS
Sociological: SOCIAL WORK ABSTRACTS, SOCIOFILE, SOCIOLOGICAL ABSTRACTS, SOCIAL SCIENCE ABSTRACTS, ANTHRO-POLOGICAL INDEX

Today, while it is possible for a library to purchase just a single data base, most libraries have found it better for them to purchase library literary searching services from vendors who have constructed searching systems that include many data bases. Libraries often purchase services from several vendors, but the prices of the vendors vary significantly, and most libraries will not have all vendor search systems. Some of the vendors have developed their own search systems, while others have focused more on providing access to existing systems. Many have a novice searching system for the people who don't know quite what they are looking for, as well as an advanced searching system for researchers who have a well-focused notion of what they need. Most of the sites contain both professional, scholar information as well as information more suitable to the lay or public audience. Frequently, the sites may have 'hot links' to other useful data sites, where you can click on a key word that takes you directly to another site that may also contain relevant information on an associated topic. Some of the most common vendor systems are: LEXIS NEXIS UNIVERSE, which is perhaps the most comprehensive, full-text vendor with hundreds of sites; EBSCO, which provides full texts in the areas of business, medicine, and the social sciences, Silver Platter, another data base that contains scholarly information, particularly Social Work Abstracts, MLA, Criminal Justice Abstracts, and PsycINFO. InfoTrac Web provides full text data bases in business, medicine, and general subject news, OCLC's First Search has many licensed data bases under their umbrella, and Dialogue @ CARL is another widely used vendor. Originally, Dialogue was the primary search device used by librarians, but today has a command language that provides access to hundreds of data bases for both the public and the professional.

Let's pretend that you are interested in researching summer camps for children. If you plug in the words 'summer camp', you may get thousands of hits that range from articles about homesickness, advertisements about where to send kids to camps, guidelines of the American Camping Association, or editorials about the need to do background checks of camp counselors. But if you are specifically interested in 'psychological adjustments of children to camp', it would be more appropriate to search in a library data base that had a specific focus on psychological issues of children, such as Sociofile, Social Work Abstracts, Psycinfo, or Mental Health Abstracts. If you are interested only in peer-reviewed journal articles, then you could click the 'advanced search' mode and 'peer reviewed' notation in order to reduce the total number of hits and get only hits that pertain directly to your topic of interest.

Most libraries have on-line systems that help teach you how to best use the Internet or the library searching systems. Some of these include: Cornell University Mann Library Gateway: Principles of Web Searching; Harvard University Library: Internet Searching Tools, Yale University Library: Internet Search Engines; Search Engine Watch, an authoritative guide to searching the Internet search engines; and Salem State College Library: Quick Tips for Using Web Search Tools.

SEARCH ENGINES

Finding information on the Internet requires that you use a search engine to locate it. All search engines are not created equal. Some are better for one thing than another. In general, search engines market themselves as hubs or web portals, where people arrive at the web to obtain information about most any subject. There are many different search engines, and new ones coming on board every day. Therefore, the list we provide here will not be comprehensive by the time you are thumbing through it. However, it will give you a very good starting place to know where to look. Each search engine will have its own peculiarities, and within a short time of surfing the net, you will inevitably find some engines that you like more than others. The other search engines may be more useful for you to use at other points in time. Some of the search engines you may want to use include: Accfind.com, All-In-One Search Page, Alta Vista, Beaucoup!, Copernicus, DejaNews, Dogpile, Excite, Hotbot, Infoseek, Internet Sleuth, Lycos, Mamma: Mother of All Search Engines, Metacrawler, MegaSearch, Multimeta: The Meta Search Engine, Northern Light, SavvySearch, Scrub the Web, Starting Point Search Engine, WebCrawler, and Yahoo.

Many of the sites found by search engines on the web pertain to organizations and commercial businesses. These are identified with the suffix. ".org" or ".com.", respectively. Most child oriented organizations, such as UNICEF or the Children's Defense Fund, have their own web sites which can be accessed. Business and commercial sites may sell products or services that could be of use to people interested in children, such as toy manufacturers. Commercial sites are not typically useful for child-oriented researchers. Organizational sites are typically more helpful. If you know the name of the organization or business, you can simply ask for it by title, similar to the same way you would have years ago at the library when using the card catalogue.

Briefly, the organizational framework of the Internet is similar to the library card catalogue systems in which one could search for the author, the title, or the subject. Millions of web sites now exist, which make it difficult for people to find all of the sites that could be relevant to their research project. As a result, search engines have been created to help the researcher to find information quickly and easily. However, all search engines are not equal. Some have broader or more specific searching capabilities. Therefore, one could plug in the term 'summer camp' in one search engine and get 27 hits, while another engine could generate

10, 763 hits. This difference results because after you input a query into a search engine website, your query is compared to and matched up with the search engine's own keyword indices. The closest matches to your search are then returned to you in a format known as hits.

Under this approach, there are two main methods of searching on an engine - "keyword" and "concept." Searching by keyword is the most commonly used form of text searching on the web. The search engines extract and index words that it recognizes as significant. You will find that words that are toward the beginning of the document and words that are continually repeated in several areas of the document have a higher chance of being extracted and indexed. Some variations to this are sites where every word in the documents are indexed, while others will only index small portions from a document. An example of this is Lycos. Lycos will index the title, headings, subheadings and the hyperlinks to other sites, with the first twenty lines of text and the hundred words that appear most often throughout the document. Infoseek on the other hand uses the complete text indexing system. It picks up every word included in the text but will exclude common words such as a, an, the, is, and, or, and www. Alta Vista says that they index all of the words including the articles of a, an, and the. Hotbot ignores stop words. Some search engines will discriminate upper case from lower case, while others store all words and do not recognize capitalization. When you search by keywords, the engines have a very difficult time distinguishing words that are spelled in the same way, but have a different meaning. An example of this would be the word 'abuse'. Different meanings would include child abuse, spouse abuse, elder abuse, animal abuse, substance abuse, or abuse of power. Words such as this will result in a mass of hits that are completely off the mark to your intended search. Some of the search engines also have problems with rules pertaining to stems. Should the extraction include the word "abuser"? There are complications when using words that have specific singular and plural meanings. One has to anticipate what to do with verb tenses which are different from the word you queried by only an ' s' or an 'ed'.

Search engines are not able to return hits on keywords that might mean the same, but are not actually entered into your search perimeters. Another frequent misconception is when you search for one word and think it will automatically give you information on words that you think are related, but the computer does not. You may ask for information on 'day care' and expect that you will also get information on 'early childhood education,' but these are two different terms.

Asking for articles on 'baby sitters' will not necessarily include documents that use the word 'au pair'. Another example of this would be searching for information on parental rights: a keyword search would not return a document that used the words 'mother' or 'father' instead of 'parental.'

The other search strategy is known as concept-based searching. In contrast to keyword search systems, concept-based search systems try to understand what you mean, not just what you type in as your key word. Under the best case scenario, concept-based search systems will return hits on documents that are related to the subject or theme you are trying to explore. It will complete this task even if the words in your query don t exactly match the words in the document. Presently, Excite is the best known, general concept search engine site on the web which uses the concept based searching approach.

Concept-based searching is also known as clustering. In simplest terms, this means that words are compared to, and grouped with, other words found close by. How does this work? The answer to that question is not a simple one we can explore here. Many of the clustering systems are highly complex and rely on sophisticated linguistic and artificial intelligence theory. However, Excite uses a numerical technique. Their software determines query meaning by calculating the frequency of certain important words. If several words or phrases which have been tagged to signal a certain idea appear close to one another in a text, the search engine will conclude, using statistical analysis, that the document is about a particular subject. The word 'growth' is a good example to use. When it is used in a medical or health context, odds are it would appear with such words as 'weight', 'height', or other physical development. On the other hand if the word 'growth' were to appear in context with the words 'self-esteem', 'cognitive maturity', or 'emotional adjustment' of a child, there would be a different context derived, and the search engine would return hits on the subject of psychological functioning. While concept-based indexing is a great idea in theory, it seldom works smoothly in real live practice. Your best results from concept-based indexing will come from entering a lot of words. You should also make sure that all the words infer the meaning of the concept you are searching for.

Refining the Electronic Search

Though there is always an exception to every rule, most sites offer two different types of searches - the basic search and the refined search. If you want to use the basic search option, you would enter a keyword without obtaining any of the additional menu options that are available to you. Even though the term basic is used, basic searches can be quite complex, so don't let the word deceive you.

If you wish to refine your options, you will find that your choices vary quite broadly from search engine to search engine. Some of the possible options may include the ability to search for more than one word, to be able to weigh one search term more than another, and to exclude words that might confuse the search engine. You may be able to limit your search to proper names, phrases, or words within a certain location from other search terms. Other choices may include giving you the ability to specify the form you would like your results to appear to you, and restrictions on certain fields within the Internet. This terminology is often referred to as Boolean operations. Below is a list of Boolean operators to refine your search. Once again, not all search engines allow you to use these terms, but you will find that a majority of them do.

And

This means that all the terms you specify must appear in the documents. Let's say you were interested in how many children get sick as a result of exposure to lead paint. In asking the computer, you would need to word it: children AND exposure to lead paint AND disease. You would want to use this when you wanted to exclude more common hits that are not important to your search.

Or

This means that at least one of the words you specify must appear in the documents you are searching for. If you were investigating physically and sexually abused children, you would have to ask: child abuse, physical OR sexual. Asking for either or both words would increase the number of hits; you wouldn't want to use this when you wanted to tightly limit your search.

Not

This means that at least one of the words you specify cannot appear in the document. Let's say you want to know about teens who are abused, not teens who are identified as abusers: abuse AND teens, NOT perpetrators. You would use this when you wanted to limit results and can anticipate hits you don't want.

+ And -

You will find that some search engines use the symbols of + and - instead of Boolean operators to include and exclude certain terms. + would equal "and" or "or", while - would equal "not".

Near

This means that the words you enter must be within a certain number of words of each other.

Followed By

This means that one word must be directly followed by another.

Adj

This means adjacent. It serves the same function as FOLLOWED BY.

Phrases

You will find that the ability to search by phrases is a very important option in a search engine. If the search engine allows, it will require you to enclose the phrase in quotation marks. And example of this would be: "I think, therefore I am", or in the case of child abuse, "the battered child syndrome".

Capitalization

You need to be especially aware of this when searching for proper names of people, companies, or products. You will find in English that many words are both used as proper and common nouns. Examples of this are, Bill, bill, Gates, gates, Oracle, oracle, Lotus, lotus, Digital, digital, and so on.

For further information on specific search engine queries, use their help files which are located on the individual search engine home page.

Relevancy Rankings

Another feature most search engines provide is confidence or relevancy rankings. This is seen when they return the list of hits to you. The list of hits are arranged according to the confidence level the search engine has in relevancy to matching with your query. Often, the results will seem completely irrelevant to the query. The reason why this happens is because the search engine technology has not reached the point where humans and computers interact well enough to communicate on the same level. You will find that most of the search engines will use search term frequency as a main way of determining whether or not a document is considered to be relevant. Let's use the word "tantrums". If it appears multiple times in a web document, it is rational to assume that the document will contain some useful information. Therefore a document that has the word tantrums repeated many times is more likely to turn up at the top of your hit list. On the other hand, if the word you use is a common word or a word that has many meanings, you might end up with a lot of unrelated hits.

Some of the better, more user-friendly search engines will consider not only the frequency but also the positioning of the keywords to prioritize relevancy. They follow the reasoning that if the keyword or words appear in the beginning of the document, or in the headers of the document, it increases the chances that the document is relevant. Lycos will rank its hits according to how many times your keywords appear in their indices of the document and in which fields they appear in. It will also take into advisement whether or not the hits that match up are regularly linked to other documents on the Web. If other people regard them to be important, then maybe you should too.

When you use search engines such as Alta Vista, use the advanced query form. You will be able to assign relevance weighs to your query terms prior to proceeding with your search. This will take some getting used to, but with practice, it will basically allow you to have greater influence on the results that come back to you. As you become a competent search engine user, relevancy ranking will become critical for you. As the immense volume of information on the web grows, relevancy ranking will become more critical. Most of us don't have the time to surf through oceans of hits to determine which hyperlink we should actually take time to explore. The more accurate the relevancy ranking results are, the less time we have to spend sifting through useless hits.

Examples of Commonly Used Search Engines

In order to give you some sense of how the search engines vary, we have provided five different examples. These examples come from of the more commonly used search engines. However, you should investigate all the engines and determine for yourself which is best for you.

Alta Vista: http//www.altavista.com

Alta Vista is one of the fastest and most powerful search engines on the Internet today. It has enough search options to perform extremely complex searches. The only problem you will find is that you have to answer all the options. If you plan on doing a lot of Web searching in the future, you will find that once you have mastered Alta Vista, you will be glad you took the extra time to do so.

Search options: Advanced or simple, refining search.
Type of Search: Keyword
Searches Domains of: Web, Usenet
Results posted as: First few lines of the document.
Ranking of relevance: Number of times your searched word(s) appears in document, placement it appears in document, and closeness of repeated word(s) searched.

Search options: AND, OR, NOT, NEAR. It Permits backwards searching. You can determine the weight of each word in your search. You can determine placement of your searched word(s) in the document. The more options you use, the better your search results will be.

Engine help files: Very thorough, but very confusing. There is too much information tossed at you without much clarity and explanation of the options.

Reasons to use: Alta Vista provides quick searches and recognizes capitalization and proper nouns. It has one of the largest data bases which allows you to find things you would not find elsewhere. It searches both the Web and Usenet. You can search both words and phrases. You can translate your search results into several languages.

Reasons not to use: Search results will frequently list same site too often. Frequent, unexplainable relevancy rankings.

Excite: http://www.excite.com

Excite likes to call itself the intelligent search engine. It rates itself highly because Excite uses a concept based indexing. Unless I missed out on a major advancement in artificial intelligence, its premise comes from a masterful use of statistics. Excite is a favorite search tool for many people.

Search options: Simple, refining search
Type of Search: Keyword and concept
Searches Domains of: Web, Usenet, and classified ads
Results posted as: Sort by site and summaries
Ranking of relevance: Provides confidence percentiles
Search options: AND, OR, NOT, and + and -
Engine help files: Excellent, includes handbook for explanation
Reasons to use: It contains a large index. Excite provides excellent summaries. It highlights the most relevant sentences in the document. You can choose how to view your hits.
Reasons not to use: Excite will not provide the size or format of the hits it returns to you. Neither does it provide the total number of hits.

Infoseek: http://infoseek.com

Search options: It is powerful, but simple.
Type of search: Keyword

Searches Domains of: Web, Usenet, Usenet FAQs, Reviews, Topics
Results posted as: Presents the first 30-100 words of the document
Ranking of relevance: Provides a number score based on how many times the word or words appear
Search options: Capitalization, Phrases, + and -
Engine help files: Good, and useful information provided
Reasons to use: Infoseek provides reliable, flexible, and above all, fast searching. It has good output information that provides the URL, the size of the document and a relevancy score. It will also allow you to see similar topic pages. It provides full text indexing and allows for capital letters and phrases.
Reasons not to use: None comes to mind

Lycos: http://www.lycos.com

Search options: Advanced or basic
Type of Search: Keyword, image, sound
Searches Domains of: Web, Usenet, News, Stocks, Weather, Multimedia
Results posted as: Presents the first 100 words, you can choose summary, full results or short version.
Ranking of relevance: Does not provide this option
Search options: Full Boolean
Engine help files: Easy to understand, graphical help, good, informative
Reasons to use: Lycos has a very large data base. It provides the date and size of the document. It also provides the number of times a document has been contacted.
Reasons not to use: Does not provide relevancy rankings.

HotBot: http://www.hotbot.com

Search options: Expert, modified, simple
Type of Search: Keyword
Searches Domains of: Web
Results posted as: Relevancy, URL
Ranking of relevance: Number of times words appear in document and placement of words in document.
Search options: Phrase, person Boolean, date, media types
Engine help files: A FAQ to answer questions, but is quite vague

Reasons to use: Fresh, lively, hip site. HotBot is very fast, because of its use of parallel processing which distributes the work over several work stations. **Reasons not to use:** Some search limitations, help files aren't very helpful, some complaints about the background color.

There are other Search Directories that you may find helpful. These include Argus Clearinghouse, a subject director, Librarian Index to the Internet, an extensive subject directory produced by public librarians in California; Magellan, a subject based directories with Web reviews and a censored category; the World Wide Web Virtual Library, which is the oldest subject directory maintained by experts in each field; The Mining Company, a subject based maintained by experts in the field, and the Internet Resources Meta-Index, which is a loosely categorized meta-index of resource directories and indices available on the Internet. There are also Image Specific Search Tools you may want to use. These include, but are not limited to: Amazing Picture Machine, Image Finder, Lycos, and WebSeer.

New search engines and web sites open daily. Therefore, it is important that when you are is conducting research that you are willing to assume a Star Trek mentality, where you are willing to dig into new, uncharted territory on a regular basis. It is also necessary that you realize that while the electronic medium is the way of researching for the future, it has certain limitations today.

There are thousands of web sites and data sources about children that a researcher may want to access. Official government positions, policies, programs, and statistics are often very useful, since they represent the governmental view of the state of children. These will be reviewed next, followed by web sites created by other organizations that are concerned about children's issues.

Chapter 4

FEDERAL GOVERNMENT RESOURCES

The data on which decisions are made about children's programming often are either collected by, or housed by, the United States government. There are many different federal governmental departments that pertain to children, and each of the departments may have multiple divisions or subdivisions that are relevant to doing research about children. Therefore, it is useful to get an overview of how some of the child-centered government departments are related. Figure 1 provides a general overview of some of the major departments.

These departments have their own websites and links to other departments. Most of the sites included here are of different government departments, such as the U.S. Department of Health and Human Services or the U.S. Department of Labor. There may be separate divisions, such as the Children's Bureau. Other sites are federal resources that disseminate information - in the case of Fedstats, statistics from more than 70 U.S. Federal government sites can be obtained. In general, federal websites offer a wide range of information and reports to aid researchers, policy makers, and program developers. Federal electronic resources have been divided by: legislative branch resources, executive branch resources, and government directories. If you are looking for information about what has been done, what is currently being done, and what will be done in the near future, federal government sites are essential resources.

LEGISLATIVE BRANCH RESOURCES

Member and Committee Information of Congress. http://clerkweb.house.gov/mbrcmtee/mbrcmtee.htm

This official federal government site contains congressional information including an alphabetical list of members with state and district information, a members telephone directory, a list of members by state, committee assignments, Senate information, U.S. House of Representatives Documents, mailing labels, and links to other Congressional sites. Laws that pertain to children and youth may be heard by certain House or Senate committees, so it is important to know which members comprise each committee. Committees that are of particular importance to children include: Appropriations; Labor, Health and Human Services and Education; Early Childhood, Youth and Families; and Criminal Justice, Drug Policy and Human Resources.

National Conference of State Legislatures. http://www.ncsl.org.

On the state level, each state is comprised of senators and representatives. This site provides information about each of the 50 state legislatures and provides comprehensive information and research on critical state issues, including issues that pertain to children. They have publications on charter schools, early childhood education, school violence, reforming juvenile justice, foster care, child abuse and neglect, child care, youth at risk, weapons, violence prevention, family preservation, family support, child health care, and a book summarizing laws affecting children and families enacted in 50 states. It also has data bases such as a Health Policy Tracking Service, a list of state legislatures, information on state-federal relations, a press room, and an opportunity to search the site for specific information. To contact:

National Conference of State Legislatures
444 North Capitol St., NW Suite 515
Washington, D.C. 20001
Tel: (202) 624-5400
Fax: (202) 737-1069

National Governors' Association. http://www.nga.org

This is a national bipartisan organization of the nation's governors that gives them a forum to discuss issues of public policy, provide assistance in solving state focused problems, and information on state innovations and practices. This site contains information about each of the governors, legislative updates, information about current issues, a press room, a bookstore, an organizational chart, and other on-line resources including reports, documents, and publications. Some of their child-specific information on their Child and Social Services site include foster care, teen pregnancy, welfare, meeting needs of out-of-school youth, responsible fatherhood, youth violence, youth crime, education, homelessness, as well as reports such as "Our Babies, Our Future", "Children: Problems and Solutions". To contact:

National Governors' Association
Hall of States
444 North Capital Street
Washington, D.C. 20001-1512
Tel: (202) 624-5300

THOMAS: Legislative information on the Internet. http://thomas.loc.gov

A site named in honor of Thomas Jefferson, it provides full text access to current bills under consideration in the U.S. House of Representatives and the Senate. This site also offers access to historical documents, Committee information, and information about the Legislative process. Many bills pertain directly, or indirectly, to infants, children, youth, and families.

U.S. House of Representatives Home Page. http://www.house.gov.

This site provides information about House operations, a House directory, access to information about bills and resolutions being considered by congress, a way to identify and contact an individuals representative, access to U.S. Federal statutes by subject, House organizations, commissions, and task forces, and a media gallery. If one wants to know what child oriented bills are pending in the House of Representatives, voting record, or if one wants to make their position known to their representative, this site can be useful.

U.S. Senate World Wide Web Server. http://www.senate.gov

This site contains information about Senate history and procedures, and gives a recent account of legislative actions, activities, Committee information, and

Senator information and voting records. It is possible to search for a specific bill by number or keyword, and access Senate information by state. For instance, by entering "children" as the keyword, over 50 different bills, ranging from children's health to child protection to homelessness, the Children's Environmental Protection Act or the Abducted Young Adults Act can be accessed.

EXECUTIVE BRANCH RESOURCES

Federal Communications Commission. http://www.fcc.gov
This site contains information about the FCC's programs and initiatives, including **LearnNet**, which discusses the importance of technology in schools and libraries. In addition there is a Health and TV page that contains information about educational TV and the V-Chip.

Federal Office of Child Support Enforcement. http://www.acf.dhhs.gov
This website is part of the Administration for Children and Families, which is part of the Department of Health and Human Services. It provides information about child support enforcement policies within different states, child support financing consultations, recent news about child support, reports, publications, and resources, policy documents including comments on the proposed rules, and links to other related websites. You can contact the OCSE directly through the website.

Library of Congress. http://www.loc.gov
This website offers library services, research tools, exhibitions, and an extensive listing of catalogs as well as an on-line exhibitions gallery, research services, and special sections for children, disabled, researchers, and publishers. It also includes a new site for "Kids & Families." This is a valuable site for all child oriented researchers! To contact:
  The Library of Congress
  101 Independence Ave. S.E.
  Washington, D.C. 20540
  Tel: (202) 707-5000

Military Child Development Program. http://dticaw.dtic.mil/milchild/model. html and the National Clearinghouse for the Military Child Development Program

Part of the Department of Defense, this program is the largest corporate-sponsored child care program in the country. The program serves over 200,000 children daily at over 300 locations worldwide. Military child care is provided in approximately 800 child development centers, school-age care facilities, and 9,700 licensed family child care homes. This website contains information about the Child Development Program, a child care library, a directory of child care centers, a clearinghouse, information about child abuse prevention and the components of quality. Also included in this site is a history of the program, policy information, and the results of two recent studies of the Child Development Program.

U.S. Census Bureau. http://www.census.gov

This site provides social, demographic, and economic information about the population. Searches can be done by state or by subjects listed from "A to Z". There is also a product catalog, links to related and minority sites, and a number of reports that can be downloaded. The Census data can provide detailed information about characteristics and compositions of children and their families across the nation, which can assist researchers in making planning, program, and policy decisions.

U.S. Consumer Product Safety Commission. http://www.cpsc.gov

It is a federal regulatory agency that helps to reduce injuries or deaths from consumer products. The website provides a library, information about the agency, business information, recall information, and reports on unsafe products. For instance, baby cribs, playpens, swings, car seats and toys are scrutinized to make sure they are safe when used by children. If one has concerns or questions about the safety of an item, this is the place to go! Also, the site contains a section called **Kidd Safety** that provides information about consumer product safety specifically for children in a game-type format.

U.S. Department of Agriculture. http://www.usda.gov/

The Department of Agriculture includes child and adult care food program and women, infants, and children. This site contains a wealth of information about the USDA's programs and agencies as well as an option to search the site for information and reports. It specifically addresses nutrition at school, what kinds of foods children should be eating - and avoiding, cooperation extension programs, which run 4-H programs, camps, and other family and child centered programs, and descriptions of expenditures on children by families, etc. It also has a child-friendly "USDA for Kids" site.

Children, Youth, and Families At Risk (CYFAR) Initiative Homepage. http://www.4h-usa.org/4h/cyfar/cyfar.htm.

This site is sponsored by the US Department of Agriculture. Through an annual Congressional appropriation for the National Children, Youth and Families at Risk (CYFAR) Initiative, funding is allocated to Land Grant University Extension Services for community-based programs for at-risk children and their families. Since 1991, the CYFAR Initiative has supported programs in more than 500 communities in 49 states. The CYFAR Initiative is based on research on effective programs for at-risk youth and families and on the human ecological principle of working across the lifespan in the context of the family and community. To assure that critical needs of children and families are met, CYFAR supports comprehensive, intensive, community-based programs developed with active citizen participation in all phases. The initiative promotes building resiliency and protective factors in youth, families and communities.

U.S. Department of Education. http://www.ed.gov

This site contains a wealth of information related to education including funding opportunities, financial aid information, research and statistics, programs and services. It also contains a list of publications and products, such as the ERIC data base, and reports on child development, charter schools, class size, safety, curriculum, after school programs, and almost everything that educators need to address. Some of the publications available through this site include the department wide initiatives for 2000, the special education and individuals with disabilities act, and elementary and secondary education and early childhood reports. The department of education's budget and links to other sites are also available. To contact:

U.S. Department of Education
400 Maryland Ave., SW
Washington, D.C. 20202-4098
Tel: (800) USA-LEARN
E-Mail: CustomerService@met.ed.gov

National Center for Education Statistics. http://nces.ed.gov
This website is part of the U.S. Department of Education and provides a large amount of statistics relating to education. The site includes a electronic catalog of the most recently released publications and data products, surveys and program areas, an encyclopedia of statistics, fast facts, and a special section for kids to search for schools and colleges. Some of their statistics include educational projections through 2008, youth indicators, and information on the condition of public and private education. Through the Common Core of Data (CCD) survey national, state, and local data on public elementary/secondary education is collected. Important additions to NCES' data collection programs in the last decade include the Schools and Staffing Survey, the Private School Universe Survey, and the National Household Education Survey. If you're interested in children's education, this site is a must!

U.S. Department of Health and Human Services. http://www.os.dhhs.gov/
This is the government's principal agency for protecting the health of all Americans and provides services for the many populations, including children. Some of its child specific agencies include: Administration for Children and Families (ACF), Centers for Disease Control and Prevention (CDC), National Institutes of Health (NIH), and Substance Abuse and Mental Health Services Administration (SAMHSA). The Department of Health and Human Services is designed to protect the health of all Americans and provide essential human services, especially for those who are least able to help themselves. It includes more than 300 programs, including research, immunization services, Medicaid, financial assistance for low-income families, child support enforcement, maternal and infant health, Head Start, preventing child abuse and domestic violence, and substance abuse treatment and prevention. HHS is the largest grant making agency in the federal government, providing 60,000 grants per year. This website provides extensive information about current issues and programs for children. It

also overviews current research, policy information, employee information, and has links to other HHS agencies. The HHS headquarters is located at:
Hubert H. Humphrey Building
200 Independence Ave., SW
Washington, DC 20201

Administration for Children and Families. http://www.acf.dhhs.gov/programs/acyf/

The Administration on Children, Youth and Families (ACYF) administers the major Federal programs that support: social services that promote the positive growth and development of children and youth and their families; protective services and shelter for children and youth in at-risk situations; child care for working families and families on public assistance; and adoption for children with special needs. These programs provide financial assistance to States, community-based organizations, and academic institutions to provide services, carry out research and demonstration activities and undertake training, technical assistance, and information dissemination. Within the ACF is the Administration on Children, Youth and Families, which is divided into four bureaus: ChildCare Bureau, Children's Bureau, Family and Youth Services Bureau, and Head Start Bureau. The ACYF also provides research demonstration and evaluation. The website offers a wealth of information about ACYF programs and research outcomes.

Child Care Bureau. http://www.acf.dhhs.gov/programs/ccb

The Child Care Bureau is part of the Administration for Children and of the U.S. Department of Health and Human Services and administers federal funds to states to assist low income families in accessing child care. The Child Care Bureau is dedicated to enhancing the quality, affordability, and supply of child care available for all families. The Child Care Bureau administers Federal funds to States, Territories, and Tribes to assist low income families in accessing quality child care for children while parents work or participate in education or training. This website contains the CCB's current initiatives, policy and funding announcements, current research, links to related sites and the National Child Care Information Center, information about the Child Care Partnership Project, and an organizational structure chart.

Children's Bureau. http://www.acf.dhhs.gov/programs/cb/

The Children's Bureau is part of the Administration on Children, Youth and Families and is responsible for assisting states in the delivery of child welfare services. This website contains information about child abuse, foster care, and adoption as well as a number of reports on child abuse and neglect and a description of current initiatives and programs. For instance, its report on Child Maltreatment: Reports From the States to the National Child Abuse and Neglect Data System provide useful statistics such as a million children in the US were found to have substantiated cases of child abuse. This site also contains information about state grant programs and discretionary grant programs.

Families and Youth Services Bureau. http://www.acf.dhhs.gov/programs /fysb

This organization is a part of the U.S. Department of Health and Human Services and provides national leadership on youth issues and assists individuals and organizations provide effective and comprehensive services for youth in at-risk situations. The mission of the Family and Youth Services Bureau (FYSB) is to provide national leadership on youth issues and to assist individuals and organizations in providing effective, comprehensive services for youth in at-risk situations and their families. A primary goal of FYSB programs is to provide positive alternatives for youth, ensure their safety, and maximize their potential to take advantage of available opportunities. This site contains information about their programs, special sections for children about running away, policy and funding announcements, publications on a variety of topics including teen pregnancy, dealing with adolescence. It also contains child health insurance information and has links to related government sites.

Head Start Bureau. http://www2.acf.dhhs.gov/programs/hsb/

Head Start is a child development program that has served low-income children and their families since 1965. Head Start is one of the remaining War on Poverty Programs - it continues to exist because of its successes in helping low income children to be competitive when they enter school. This website is a resource for Head Start service providers, parents, volunteers, community organizations, and others interested in Head Start. The site contains news and initiatives, a list of programs, research and development, funding opportunities, regulations, publications, directories, a list of grantees, and income guidelines.

Research Demonstration and Evaluation. http://www2.acf.dhhs.gov/ programs/hsb/core/

This branch of the Administration for Children and Families is responsible for the coordination of social and behavioral research and evaluation activities. The Commissioner's Office of Research and Evaluation (CORE), located within the office of the Administration on Children, Youth and Families (ACYF) Commissioner, is the unit responsible for providing scientific consultation, coordination, executive direction, and support for the implementation of short- and long-term research agendas within and across the four Bureaus of ACYF: Child Care Bureau, Children's Bureau, Family and Youth Services Bureau; and Head Start Bureau. This website contains publications, a guide to evaluation, and Head start research, child care research, child welfare and evaluation activities, child abuse and neglect research, and family and youth services research.

Agency for Health Care Policy and Research. http://www.ahcpr.gov

This is the lead agency charged with supporting research designed to improve the quality of health care, reduce its cost, and broaden access to essential services. This website contains funding opportunities, research findings on a variety of health care related topics including children, clinical information, and data. It has a specific child health section that includes a wide range of projects and reports, including Health Care of America's Young, $9.1 Million Awarded for Studies Designed to Improve Health Care for Low-income Children, $2.1 Million in Grants Awarded to Study Child Mental Health Conditions, Children's Death Rates Fall Sharply in Intensive Care Units, Less Expensive But Equally Effective Antibiotics To Treat Ear Infections Could Reduce Medical Expenditures, Pediatric Emergency Medicine, Caring for Children With Asthma, children's health insurance programs and other information about children's health.

Center for Disease Control and Prevention. http://www.cdc.gov

The Centers for Disease Control and Prevention (CDC), located in Atlanta, Georgia, USA, is an agency of the Department of Health and Human Services. Its mission is to promote health and quality of life by preventing and controlling disease, injury, and disability. The CDC includes 11 Centers, Institute, and Offices, including the National Center for Health Statistics, National Center for Chronic Disease Prevention and Health Promotion, Office of Genetics and Disease Prevention, National Center for HIV, STD, and TB Prevention, National

Center for Injury Prevention and Control and the National Immunization Program, all which could pertain to infants, children, and youth. This site provides health data and statistics, information about grants other funding opportunities, an opportunity to search for information on a variety of health related topics, links to other sites, and an opportunity to subscribe to their health publications.

Department of Health and Human Services Data Council. http://aspe.os. dhhs.gov/datacncl

This organization coordinates all health and non-health data collection and analysis activities of the Department of Health and Human Services, including an integrated health data collection strategy, coordination of health data standards, and health information and privacy policy activities. Many of its reports pertain to the health of infants, children, and youth, and those agencies which serve them.

Girl Power. http://www.health.org/gpower/

Girl Power is a national public education campaign sponsored by the Department of Health and Human Services geared towards 9 to 14 year old girls. Girl Power! seeks to reinforce and sustain these positive values among girls by targeting health messages to the unique needs, interests, and challenges. This website contains information for girls and parents, and press releases. Some of the research reports obtained via Girl Power are: girls in technology, relationship between sports and teen pregnancy, gender inequality in schools, and girls substance abuse.

Health Care Financing Administration. http://www.hcfa.gov

This is the federal agency that administers the Medicare, Medicaid, and Child Health Insurance Programs. HCFA provides health insurance for over 74 million Americans through Medicare, Medicaid and SCHIP (State Child Health Insurance Program). Medicaid and SCHIP are primary health care programs used by low income children. This site contains information and reports on these health care programs, information on projects and initiatives of the HCFA, statistics and data, research information, an information clearinghouse, laws and regulations. Its Insure Kids Now program attempts to get children enrolled into the SCHIP program so that all low income children can get the health care they need.

Health Resources and Services Administration. http://www.hrsa.dhhs.gov

The Health Resources and Services Administration (HRSA) directs national health programs that improve the Nation's health by assuring equitable access to comprehensive, quality health care for all. HRSA works to improve and extend life for people living with HIV/AIDS, provide primary health care to medically underserved people, serve women and children through State programs, and train a health workforce that is both diverse and motivated to work in underserved communities. This organization directs the national health programs which improve the health of the Nation by insuring quality health care to underserved, vulnerable, and special need populations. This website contains information about their Focus on Child Health initiative, grants and contracts, budget and appropriations information, state profiles, HRSA grants preview information, and an overview of programs. One of the HRSAs major programs is the Maternal and Child Health Bureau. Charged with the primary responsibility for promoting and improving the health of our Nation's mothers and children, the Maternal and Child Health Bureau (MCHB) draws upon nearly a century of commitment and experience. Early efforts are rooted in MCHB's predecessor, the Children's Bureau, established in 1912. Today MCHB manages The Maternal and Child Health Services Block Grant (Title V), FY' 99 budget-$700 million, The Healthy Start Initiative (Public Health Service Act), FY'99 budget-$105 million, The Emergency Medical Services for Children Program (Public Health Service Act), FY'99 budget-$15 million, and the Abstinence Education Program.

National Committee on Vital and Health Statistics. http://www.ncvhs.hhs.gov

This committee provides advice and assistance to the Department of Health and Human Services and serves as a forum for interaction with interested private sector groups on a variety of key health data issues. The NCVHS serves as the statutory public advisory body to the Secretary of Health and Human Services in the area of health data and statistics. It collects data on births, infant mortality, child and infant disease, teen pregnancy, and other information that researchers about child health issues will want to know.

National Institute of Health. http://www.nih.gov

NIH is one of eight agencies under the US Department of Health and Human Services. It contains 25 different divisions, including the National Institute of Child Health and Human Development and the National Institute of Mental Health, both of which are critically involved in supporting children's issues. It provides support to researchers, as well as program development, medical schools, hospitals, and public education. This site contains an overview of this government agency as well as a calendar of events, health publications, clinical trials, a guide to diseases under investigation at NIH, information about grants including application kits and research contracts, on-line journals, and on-line research labs. To contact:
Harold Varmus, Director
National Institute of Health
Bethesda, MD 20892

National Institute of Child Health and Human Development. http://www.nichd.nih.gov/

This organization is part of the National Institute of Health and conducts and supports laboratory, clinical, and epidemiological research on the reproductive, neurobiology, developmental, and behavioral processes that determine and maintains the health of children, families, adults, and populations. This site contains information about what's new with the NICHD, funding by NICHD, intramural research, epidemiology statistics and prevention, publications clearinghouse, research resources, and employment and fellowship opportunities. The NICHD also sponsors the Center for Research for Mothers and Children. This site contains a special section for child researchers, and publications on topics such as child well being, adolescent health, infant health, as well as other information and links related to this center.

Office of Disease Prevention and Health Promotion. http://odphp.osophs.dhhs.gov/

This government agency works to strengthen the disease prevention and health promotion priorities of the Department of Health and Human Services and works closely with the Department. This site contains on-line publications including the Guide to Clinical Preventive Services, announcements of upcoming events, and links to other related sites. It established the Healthy People 2010 guidelines, a handbook for prevention services, and publications of the National Clearinghouse on Children and Youth.

Office of Health Policy. http://aspe.os.dhhs.gov/health/hphome.htm
This site is part of the Department of Health and Human Services, it offers on-line research on health policy and child health, especially children's health insurance issues. It focuses on policy planning and coordination, policy and budget analysis, review and formulation of legislation and regulations, and the conduct and coordination of research and evaluation on issues relating to health policy. Considering 11 million children are estimated to have no health insurance, the OHP has an important role to play in helping to create policies so that all children receive the health care they need.

Substance Abuse and Mental Health Services Administration. http://www.samhsa.gov
This agency is part of the U.S. Department of Health and Human Services and works to provide substance abuse and mental health services. This site contains substance abuse and mental health information, statistics on adolescent substance use, grants, adolescent and child substance abuse treatment and prevention program information, links to six special offices that focus on specific areas such as the Office of Managed Care and the Office on Aids and a clearinghouse house. There are also news releases, an opportunity to search the site for specific information and media services that could be of help to those wishing to prevent substance abuse in children.

Center for Mental Health Services. http://www.mentalhealth.org/cmhs
This agency is part of the Substance Abuse and Mental Health Services Administration and leads federal efforts to treat mental illnesses and increase the quality and range of treatment, rehabilitation, and support services for people with mental illnesses, their families, and communities. Teen substance abuse prevention and mental health is a particular focus. This site contains information on the children's campaign including annual reports and description of emergency services, community supports, mental health statistics, funding, and much more.

Youth Info. http://youth.os.dhhs.gov

This website is designed by the Department of Health and Human Services to provide current information about a range of issues confronting adolescents and their families. Included on the website is a profile of America's youth, reports and publications, resources for parents, speeches on youth topics, related websites, and a message from Donna Shalala. You can contact Youth Info at: E-Mail: youth@osaspe.dhhs.gov

U.S. Department of Housing and Urban Development. http://www.hud.gov

This site contains information about HUD's programs and initiatives including children's health and community safety. HUD is responsible for many of the programs for homeless children, youth, and their families. There is also a special section for kids and a comprehensive site tour as well as links to other federal websites. The kid site attempts to help children understand about the homeless and empower them to be helpful citizens.

U.S. Department of Justice. http://www.usdoj.gov

This site contains information about the organization, publications and documents, community supports and grants, and fugitives and missing persons. There is a special section on justice for youth and kids that has information on how kids can help prevent crime, civil rights, Internet do's and don'ts with sections for parents and teachers. For instance, there is a section on child abduction which focuses primarily on stranger abduction. However, since most child abductions are made by people whom the child knows, it is important that child sites be used in interaction with an adult whom the child trusts who can help them put the material into context. The site possibly has more utility for researchers who are looking for general justice information as it pertains to children.

Bureau of Justice Statistics. http://www.ojp.usdoj.gov/bjs/

This site is a component of the U.S. Department of Justice and provides statistics and information about criminal offenders, crimes and victims, and the justice system. The BJS also provides data for analysis and online access to Crime and Justice Data Abstracts and online tabulations, datasets, and codebooks. To contact the BJS:

Bureau of Justice Statistics
810 Seventh Street, NW
Washington, DC 20531
Tel: (202) 307-0765
E-Mail: askbjs@ojp.usdoj.gov

U.S. Department of Labor. http://www.dol.gov

The U.S. Department of Labor is charged with preparing the American workforce for new and better jobs, and ensuring the adequacy of America's workplaces. It is responsible for the administration and enforcement of over 180 federal statutes. These legislative mandates and the regulations produced to implement them cover a wide variety of workplace activities for nearly 10 million employers and well over 100 million workers, including protecting workers' wages, health and safety, employment and pension rights; promoting equal employment opportunity; administering job training, unemployment insurance and workers' compensation programs; strengthening free collective bargaining and collecting, analyzing and publishing labor and economic statistics. This site contains information about the DOL and it's agencies, a library of information related to labor, laws and regulations, statistics and data, a news room, DOL contacts, and links to related sites. There is also a special section for children called Safe Work/Safe Kids which works to keep kids safe on the job.

Occupational Safety and Health Administration. http://www.osha.gov

This agency is part of the U.S. Department of Labor and works to save lives, prevent injuries, and protect the health of American workers. This site includes a news room, OSHA regulations, technical links and training information, and a library that contains statistics and data, manuals, and reports. It is a useful site to determine the government's priorities toward the safety of young workers.

Bureau of Labor Statistics. http://www.bls.gov

This website's part of the U.S. Department of labor and contains data, the economy at a glance, regional information, publications and research papers, surveys and programs, links to other statistical sites, and K-12 educational resources. The site includes a child-oriented section in which specific occupations are described and promoted by young workers.

U.S. Department of Transportation. http://www.dot.gov

This organization works to ensure a safe, fast, efficient, accessible, and convenient transportation system that meets our national interests and enhances our quality of life. This website includes news and events, dockets, rules, and references, program and initiative information, and research information. It specifies regulations for school buses and would be of particular use to those who transport children to and from programs.

Bureau of Transportation Statistics. http://www.bts.gov

This site is part of the U.S. Department of Transportation and contains airline information, commodity flow survey, databases, geographic information services, statistical policy and research. It also contains a child centered section to teach children about transportation and possible careers in the transportation field.

U.S. Environmental Protection Agency. http://www.epa.gov/children/

This site entitled Children's Health Protection is devoted to providing information to help protect children from environmental threats. There is information about children's health research, asthma, federal activities, international children's health, and what's new as well as a link to the main EPA website. The section on Office of Children's Health Protection and the section on Children's Environment are of use to children and those who work with kids.

The White House. http://www.whitehouse.gov and the White House for Kids. http://whitehouse.gov/WH/kids/html/kidshome.html

This site offers information about the President and Vice President, the history of the White House, and access to federal services as well as information on what's new, a virtual library of White House documents, the White House Help desk, and an interactive citizens' handbook.

GOVERNMENT DIRECTORIES

The Electronic Activist. http://www.berkshire.net/~ifas/activist/

A service of the Institute of First Amendment Studies, this is a research and educational organization focusing on the separation of church and state. Its database currently contains contact information for U.S. senators and representatives, governors, and some state legislatures, as well as a directory of e-mail addresses of congress people, state government, and media entities. This information is critical when one wants to contact people regarding child legislation.

The Federal Web Locator. http://www.infoctr.edu/fwl
Sponsored by the Villanova Center for Information Law and Policy, this site is a one stop shopping point for federal government information on the web. It has links to the judicial, legislative and executive branches of the government, federal government agencies, consortiums, and other resources. When in doubt about how to find a government agency that works on behalf of children, this site may be able to help you!

Fedstats. http://www.fedstats.gov
This site contains statistics from more than 70 U.S. Federal Government agencies. This site can be searched by agency, program, region, or topic. There are also press releases, fast facts, and additional links to related sites. It contains information about children and crime, foster care, child care, child health, and other child related information.

Fedworld. www.fedworld.gov
This site provides one stop shopping for U.S. government information, including servers, reports, a FTP site, and a Telnet site with information from over 50 agencies. This site is provided by the National Technical Information Service. It contains detailed information about child welfare, child health, education, substance abuse, family issues, and other relevant child-centered information.

Nonprofit Gateway. http://www.nonprofit.gov
This site is a network of links to Federal government information and services for nonprofit organizations. The site contains links to all the federal government departments, links to the federal agencies, browse information on the executive, legislative, and judicial branches, links to important Federal information clearinghouses and services, grant information, budgets, and management and policy resources. Searches can also be done by keyword or phrase.on more than 530,000 government web pages. This is a quick way to find child resource information.

Pavnet. http://www.pavnet.org

The Partnership Against Violence, this site is a virtual library of information about violence and youth-at-risk, representing data from seven different Federal agencies including U.S. Department of Education, Department of Justice, Department of Defense, USDA, HUD, HHS, and others. There is also a conference calendar, a user's guide, and funding information. This site can be a valuable for people who wish to prevent violence among teens. To contact:

John Gladstone
Tel: (301) 504-5462
E-Mail: jgladst@nalusda.gov

Chapter 5

CHILD POLICY

There are a variety of organizations that produce or collect information that is used to create policies on children's issues. Some of these policies are specific to one particular issue or a certain group of people; others are broad and inclusive. Policy oriented organizations are varied, with some seeking to create national or international child policies, while others develop more local policies. However, most of the web sites contained here focus on improving the national agenda for children.

Action Alliance for Children. http://www.4children.org/
This is a California based non-profit agency that provides information about the current trends and policy issues affecting children and their families. AAC publishes the *Children's Advocate* newsmagazine. In addition, the agency coordinates conferences and training courses; publishes a *Master Calendar* of events and resources; and produces videos about violence and young children.

This website offers information about the organization, membership, and subscription to the *Children's Advocate*, a statewide directory of child advocates, and links to other related websites. There is also information about internship opportunities and roundtable discussions of current policy issues affecting children. To contact the AAC write to:

Action Alliance for Children
1201 Martin Luther King Jr. Way
Oakland, CA 94612
Tel: (510) 444-7136

E-Mail: aac@4children.org

American Indian Research and Policy Institute. http://www.airpi.org
This non-profit organization serving mid west American Indian groups was founded by a group of American Indian professionals who felt the American Indian population and the wider community needed a forum to discuss the challenges of contemporary Indian life. This agency works to provide government leaders, policy makers, and the public with accurate information about the legal and political history of American Indian nations and the contemporary situation for American Indians. This site contains information about recent forums and issues that are currently being addressed, including child welfare, a list of resources, information on research projects, and links to related sites. To contact:

American Indian Research and Policy Institute
749 Simpson St.
St. Paul, MN 55104
E-Mail: airpi@baldeagle.com

American Civil Liberties Union. http://www.aclu.org
The ACLU is a nonprofit, nonpartisan, 275,000-member public interest organization devoted exclusively to protecting the basic civil liberties of all Americans, and extending them to groups that have traditionally been denied them. It is the nation's foremost advocate of individual rights and works to create legislation and provide education on a broad array of issues affecting individual freedom in the United States. This site contains information on the issues the ACLU is currently working on including drug policy, women's rights, students rights, gay and lesbian rights, privacy, free speech, cyber rights, disability rights, national security, equality, death penalty, criminal justice, reproductive rights, and much more. There is also information about what's happening with these issues in congress and the courts, a library of information and reports, and a brief history of the organization. To contact:

American Civil Liberties Union
125 Broad St., 18th Floor
New York, NY 10004-2400

American Youth Policy Forum. http://www.aypf.org
   The American Youth Policy Forum is a nonpartisan professional development organization providing learning opportunities for policymakers working on youth issues at the local, state and national levels. Forum participants include Congressional aides, officials of various federal agencies, policymakers from national non-profit associations and advocacy organizations, and state and local government officials. This site contains information about the organization, publications, forum briefs, a staff directory, trip reports, a list of past activities, people talk- a list of quotes and interviews with participants, and links to related sites. To contact:
   American Youth Policy Forum
   1836 Jefferson Place, NW
   Washington, D.C. 20036
   Tel: (202) 775-9731
   Fax: (202) 775-9733
   E-Mail: aypfy@aypf.org

Center for Child and Family Policy. http://www.pubpol.duke.edu/centers/ child/index.html
   Sponsored by Duke University, this organization works to improve children's well being through an integrated system of scientific research, debate and dissemination, public service, and teaching. The Center for Child and Family Policy hopes to bridge the gap between basic research and policy and practice. This site contains information about current research projects, a list of upcoming activities and conferences, information about classes on child policy, information about public service, debates of current policy issues, a list of faculty and staff at the Center for Child and Family Policy, and press releases. There are also links to other sites providing child policy research.

Center on Budget and Policy Priorities. http://www.cbpp.org
   This is a research organization and policy institute that conducts research and analysis on a range of government policies and programs, with an emphasis on those affecting low-income and moderate-income people. The Center specializes in research and analysis oriented toward policy decisions that policymakers face at both federal and state levels. The Center examines data and research findings and produces analyses designed to be accessible to public officials, other non-

profit organizations, and the media. This site contains publications, a number of reports that can be accessed directly, information about the Start Health Stay Health Campaign, State Fiscal Analysis, and State Policy Documentation Project, international projects, low income housing, food assistance, health, immigrants, the federal budget, state fiscal policies, safety nets, social security, and poverty and income. There is also an opportunity to search the site for specific reports and information. To contact:

Center on Budget and Policy Priorities
820 First St., NE Suite 510
Washington, D.C. 20002
Tel: (202) 408-1080
Fax: (202) 408-1056
E-Mail: bazie@cbpp.org

Chapin Hall Center for Children. http://www.chapin.uchicago.edu

This is located at the University of Chicago and is a research and development center for policies and programs that affect children, families, and communities. Chapin Hall's primary work is research that addresses two questions: (1) What does our society now do for children? and (2) What other approaches might we as a society take to meet our responsibility to children? This website contains information about the organization, downloadable publications, information about children's services, primary supports, community building, schools' connections, international projects, as well as a staff list, job opportunities, and links to other related websites.

Child Rights Information Network. http://www.crin.org

The Child Rights Information Network (CRIN) is a membership-driven organization and network of over 1,000 child rights organizations from around the world. CRIN works to improve the lives of children by promoting the UN Convention on the Rights of the Child, exchanging information about child rights, and developing networking tools and capacity building for information exchange among CRIN members. This site contains child rights publications, a calendar of events, a website directory, a tour of child rights organizations, a special section on the rights of children living with HIV/AIDS, an opportunity to search the site for specific information, and a newsletter. To contact:

Becky Purbrick

c/o Save the Children
17 Grove Lane
London, SE5 8RD, UK
Tel: 44 171 703 5400
Fax 44 171 793 7630
E-Mail: crin@pro-net.co.uk

Child Trends, Inc. http://www.childtrends.org
This is a non-partisan, non-profit research organization that studies children, youth, and families, provides technical assistance to other agencies, and provides information on public policy issues that affect children and families. Child Trends conducts basic research and evaluation studies in several critical areas including: teenage pregnancy and childbearing, the effects of welfare and poverty on children, issues related to parenting, family structure, and family processes, including fatherhood and male fertility. A highlight of this website is The Child Indicator, an online newsletter whose purpose is to communicate the major developments within each sector of the child and youth indicators field to the larger community and includes articles on projects and programs using child and youth indicators at the national, state, and community levels, with occasional reports on international projects. This website contains information about current research projects, abstracts of recent papers, a publications list, press releases, job announcements, facts-at-a-glance, and links to related websites. To contact them:
Child Trends, Inc.
4301 Connecticut Ave., NW
Washington, DC 20008
Tel: (202) 362-5580
Fax: (202) 362-5533

Child Welfare Research. http://www.childwelfare.com
This site is sponsored by the School of Public Policy and Social Research at the University of California, Los Angeles and contains the Child Welfare Review, an electronic journal that contains information about important topics in child welfare. Many of the articles are located at web sites around the world. Topics include: child abuse, foster care, welfare reform and children, child poverty and inequality, child advocacy, and child values. There is also a library containing links to major journals, a directory of email address for social work faculty, a

photo essay and poem, and links to Think Tanks and Research Organizations as well as a tutorial section on how to use the Internet. In addition, there is a link to Oxford University Press' Series in Child Welfare Practice, Policy, and Research. To contact:
>Child Welfare Research Institute
>919 Levering Ave. Suite 208
>Child Welfare Research Institute
>Los Angeles, CA 90024
>E-Mail: info@childwelfare.com

Child Welfare League of America. http://www.cwla.org
This is the nations oldest and largest national non-profit organization that develops and promotes programs and policies that serve children and families. The CWLA has over a thousand public and private member agencies. This website contains information about the organization, CWLA contacts for local areas, information about their internship program, a list of publications, information about their speakers bureau, position announcements, consultation and professional development information. The site also provides information about corporate partners and member agencies, advocacy information, a calendar of events, how to donate, current news and events that affect child welfare, and publications including the Child Welfare Journal, Children's Monitor, and Children's Voice Magazine. To contact the CWLA:
>Child Welfare League of America
>440 First Street, NW, 3rd Floor
>Washington, DC 20001-2085
>Tel: (202) 638-2952
>Fax: (202) 638-4004

Children Now. http://www.childrennow.org
This is a non-profit organization that is nationally recognized for its policy expertise and current information about the status of children, particularly children who are poor or at risk, with a special focus on California. This website contains a wealth of information about children with specific attention to media advocacy, the Internet, children's health, working families, and how to talk to children about tough issues. There are also annual statistical reviews on the status of California's children at both the state and the county level, an extensive list of links to other

websites, a number of reports and Action Guides that can be downloaded, and an occasional live webcast. To contact Children Now write to:
Children Now
1212 Broadway, 5th Floor
Oakland, CA 94612
Tel: (510) 763-2444
Fax: (510) 763-1974
E-Mail: children@childrennow.org

Coalition for America's Children. http://www.usakids.org
This organization is an alliance of national, state and local non-profit organizations working to improve the well-being of children and help create good public policy. This site, published by the Benton Foundation, includes information about the 2000 campaign "Who's for Kids and Who's Just Kidding" as well as what the latest research says about how the public views children's issues such as what adults want for working families, adult perceptions of today's youth, and a nation wide opinion poll of on those without insurance. Also found on this website is a lengthy list of publications that can be ordered, links to hundreds of member organizations and groups, information on how to join, and a link to the Missing Children HELP Center.

Committee for Economic Development. http://www.ced.org
This organization is an independent, nonpartisan, trustee-directed organization of business and education leaders dedicated to policy research on the major economic and social issues and the implementation of its recommendations by the public and private sectors. Unique among U.S. business organizations, CED offers senior executives a nonpolitical forum for exploring critical long-term issues and making an impact on U.S. policy decisions. This site contains information about the organization, a list of donors, annual reports, a news room, information about international counterparts, a list of research advisory board members, information about policy programs, publications, and an opportunity to search the site for specific information.

Common Cause. http://www.commoncause.org
Founded by John Gardner, former Secretary of Health, Education and Welfare, this is a grassroots, non-profit lobbying organization promoting open,

honest, accountable government. Common Cause regularly publishes investigative studies on the effects of money in politics and reports on a variety of ethics and integrity-in-government issues. This site contain information about the organization, articles about current policy issues listed by state, links to state and local government websites, campaign finance studies publications, and a know your congress section. Also included in this website is CauseNet, an electronic way to stay informed about how elected official stand on Common Cause issues and the Washington Watchdog, providing articles about ethics in government, corporate welfare, open government, constitutional amendments, and investigations.

Electronic Policy Network. http://epn.org/prospect.html
Sponsored by The American Prospect, this is an on-line resource for extensive research information from a variety of sources on the subjects of economics, welfare and families, and education, particularly as they relate to low income children and families. This website includes web only featured articles, interactive discussion groups, biographies and interviews, a complete archive of past issues, and information on how to subscribe.

The Future of Children. http://www.futureofchildren.org
From the Packard Foundation, *The Future of Children* is published three times a year for the purpose of disseminating timely information on major issues related to children's well-being, with special emphasis on providing objective analysis and evaluation, translating existing knowledge into effective programs and polices, and promoting constructive institutional change. Included in the site are a number of on-line journals relating to children and children's issues that are targeted for policy makers, practitioners, legislators, executives, and other professionals.

Idea Central. http://www.epn.org/ideacentral
A project of The American Prospect, is the virtual magazine of the Electronic Policy Network and provides information about current issues and public policies affecting children, families, and low income people. This website includes policy facts, pick of the week, a list of member organizations including a brief description of each organization, a list of policy jobs and internships, a list of

upcoming events, a directory of other policy resources, news releases listed by subject, and an archives listed by author.

Information Clearinghouse on Children. http://www.acusd.edu/childrens issues/

This is part of the Children's Advocacy Institute at the University of San Diego School of Law and works to provide information about children's issues, publishes reports on public policy decisions that affect children, and offers advocacy training. This website contains current reports from this and other child welfare organizations, issue alerts, commentaries, children's regulatory law reporter, advocacy information, current legislation news including pending legislation and the 1999 Children's Legislative Report Card, new releases, and links to related websites. To contact the Children's Advocacy Institute write to:

Margaret A. Dalton, J.D., Project Director
Information Clearinghouse on Children
University of San Diego School of Law
5998 Alcala Park
San Diego, CA 92110
Tel: (619) 260-4279
Fax: (619) 260-4753
E-Mail: childrensissues@acusd.edu

Institute for Research on Poverty. http://www.ssc.wisc.edu/irp/

Based at the University of Wisconsin-Madison, this is a non-profit, non partisan national center for research into the causes and consequences of poverty and social inequity in the United States. This organization is also one of the two centers designated as a National Poverty Research Center by the U.S. Department of Health and Human Services. This site contains a list of research initiatives and IRP grants, information about welfare reform in Wisconsin, the national welfare debate and the new measurement of poverty. There is also a publication section, a way to search the site for information and reports, and links to poverty related resources as well as to the University of Wisconsin at Madison. To contact: Institute for Research on Poverty:

3412 Social Science Building
1180 Observatory Dr.
Madison, WI 53706

Tel: (608) 262-6358
Fax: (608) 265-3119

Morrison Institute for Public Policy. www.asu.edu/copp/morrison
Sponsored by Arizona State University, this institute conducts research on public policy matters and informs policy makers and residents about issues of importance, and advises leaders on choices and actions. This site contains information about current research such as the Arizona Quality of Life Study, evaluation of Phoenix Head Start Program, and the Brookings Institution Metropolitan Case Study of Greater Phoenix. There are also publications on economic development, education, the environment, urban growth, social issues, government, and community participation in public affairs, a list of Morrison Institute clients, a staff directory, and links to Arizona State University School for Public Affairs and College of Public Programs. To contact:
School of Public Affairs
Arizona State University
P.O. Box 874405
Tempe, AZ 85287-4405
Tel: (480) 965-4525
Fax: (480) 965-9219

National Center for Children in Poverty. http://cpmcnet.columbia. edu/dept/nccp
This organization is sponsored by Columbia University and works to promote strategies that reduce child poverty and improve life chance of those children who are living in poverty. This site contains information related to child poverty including statistics, reports, publications, a newsletter, media resources, child poverty facts, state and local information, information child care and early education, family support programs and welfare reform, and a research forum. Also included in this website is a comprehensive program summary that discusses the nature of poverty's impact on children. To contact:
National Center for Children in Poverty
The Joseph L. Mailman School of Public Health
Columbia University
154 Haven Ave.
New York, NY 10032

Tel: (212) 304-7100
Fax: (212) 544-4200 or (212) 544-4201

National Network for Youth. http://www.nn4youth.org
This is a non-profit membership organization that informs public policy, educates the public and strengthens the field of youth work to help improve the lives of disadvantaged youth and their communities. This organization provides youth advocacy, community youth development, publications, and training and consultation for other organizations and individuals working with children. National Network for Youth is also involved with the Council on Accreditation Services for Families and Children and offers accreditation for National Network member agencies at a discounted rate. This website includes an overview of their 1999 and 2000 symposiums, featured articles, the Community Youth Development Journal, information about street work, health promotion and development, youth adult partnerships, community youth development and youth involvement and leadership. To contact the National Network for Youth:
Bob McCormick
c/o Henry S. Lehr, Inc.
3893 Adler Place
Bethlehem, PA 18017
Tel: (800) 634-8237
E-Mail: info@hslehr.com

National Partnership for Women and Families. http://www.national partnership.org
This is a non-profit organization that provides education and advocacy to promote workplace fairness, quality healthcare, and policies that help men and women meet the demands of work and family. This agency was formally known as the Women's Legal Defense League. This website contains job opportunities, a list of upcoming events, a list of publications, a video about the organization, a guide for caseworkers and others helping welfare recipients enter the workforce, information about the *Patients' Bill of Rights Act*, and information on how to get involved.

Research Forum on Children, Families, and the New Federation.
http://researchforum.org/cfm/home.cfm

This is an initiative of the National Center for Children in Poverty and the Joseph L Mailman School of Public Health at Columbia University and encourages collaborative research and informed policy on welfare reform and vulnerable populations. This site includes an on-line database that contains summaries of over 100 policy relevant research projects that examine welfare reform and the well being of low-income children and families. There is also a newsletter and links to related sites and resources.

United Way. http://www.unitedway.org

The United Way is an international, non-profit organization who's mission is to respond to and support local United Way member organizations to help increase the organized capacity for people to care for one another.

The United Way is an organization that is devoted to the needs of the youth development field and provides evaluation, research, publications, projects, funding, policy, training, and statistics. This website contains facts about the United Way, links to local and international chapters, news, information about community building, job openings, and partnerships. There is also a journal focused on community building for community leaders, fact sheets, various child development initiatives, public policy electronic resources, and an outcome measurement resource network.

The Urban Institute. http://www.urban.org

This organization is a non-profit, policy research organization that investigates social and economic problems confronting the nation and analyzes efforts to solve these problems. This site contains useful resources on policy issues and an analysis of the State Children's Health Insurance Program. There is also information about at risk teens, crime in America, welfare reform, a national survey of America's families, and other special projects. Visitor's of this site have access to research by topic and author and a number of reports on a variety of subjects as well as access to recent news articles published by the institute. To contact:

The Urban Institute
2100 M Street, NW
Washington, DC 20037

Tel: (202) 833-7200

Welfare to Work: The McKnight Foundation. http://www.mcknight.org
This private, philanthropic foundation that works to improve the quality of life for present and future generations by supporting efforts to strengthen communities, families, and individuals, particularly those in need, and by contributing to the arts, encouraging preservation of our natural environment, and promoting research in selected fields. This website provides information about the foundation, how to apply for grants, news articles, publications, and program descriptions. Special initiatives include child abuse prevention, welfare reform, and the family loan program. There is also a link their welfare to work sub site the provides a wealth of information about welfare reform including online documents and articles, news updates, Welfare to Work newsletter, a listserv links to related sites and links to partnership programs. There is also information about conferences and workshops.

Welfare Policy Center of the Hudson Institute. http://hudson.org/wpc/
This non-profit organization is a project of the Indianapolis-based Hudson Institute and is supported in part by the Lynde and Harry Bradley, W.K. Kellogg, and Annie E. Casey Foundations. It is a resource for policy makers, program administrators, the press, and works to redefine the meaning of public assistance through research, policy analysis, and technical assistance.

This site contains information about the center, articles and papers, research and projects including research on fathers and non-custodial parents, faith based organizations and welfare reform, healthcare, and a study of former welfare recipients. There is also a newsletter, a bookstore, and links to related sites.

Chapter 6

LEGAL RESOURCES

This collection of web sites provides information about children and the law, juvenile justice, child support enforcement, and other issues relating to laws, policies, and practices that effect children. An excellent site to begin research on these topics is the American Bar Association Center on Children and the Law web site which contains a wealth of information on a variety of issues concerning children and the law. The Juvenile Justice Clearinghouse from Florida State University is another excellent site to begin researching and provides extensive information on subjects relating to juvenile justice. Overall, these web sites offer comprehensive information about children and the law and many contain links to other useful web sites.

American Bar Association Center on Children and the Law.
http://www.abanet.org/child
This organization works to improve laws and policies affecting children, research and provide information on laws, policies, and practices affecting children, and increase public awareness of law and justice issues that relate to children, specifically in the areas of child abuse and neglect, child welfare, foster care, child abductions, child and adolescent health issues, substance abuse and child protection, and legal representation of children, parents, and child welfare agencies. This website contains a wealth of information about children and the law and has a number of reports and current legislation that can be downloaded. Also on the website is a list of publications and periodicals, the annual report,

internship opportunities, discussion groups, a factbook, lawyer standards, and links to other ABA sites as well as to other agency sites. To contact the ABA:
American Bar Association
750 Lake Shore Dr.
Chicago, IL 60611
Tel: (302) 988-5000
E-Mail: info@abanet.org

Association for Children for Enforcement of Support. http://www.child support-aces.org/home.html
This is a non-profit organization of parents concerned about child support issues that works to improve child support enforcement, educate parents about their legal rights, and promote public awareness about the child support issues. This website contains a list of publications including a child support reference guide, a member newsletter, access to the ACES child support hotline, statistics, current laws and actions, locating absent parents, accomplishments, and links to related government agencies. To contact the ACES call their hotline at 1 (800) 738- ACES.

Center for Law and Social Policy. http://www.clasp.org
Founded by lawyers, this non-profit organization provides education, policy research, and advocacy to improve the economic security of low-income children and families and to secure access for persons to our civil justice system. This site contains audio conferences, information on the state policy documentation project and the Project for the Future of Equal Justice, a list of publications including a documents archives, information about special initiatives, internship, job and fellowship opportunities, and links to related sites. Site visitors can also request special information from the organization via email. To contact:
The Center for Law and Social Policy
1616 P Street, NW
Suite 150
Washington, DC 20036
Tel: (202) 328-5140
Fax: (202) 328-5195

Legal Resources

Child Care Law Center. http://childcarelaw.org

This is a national, non-profit legal services organization that works to foster high quality, affordable child care, with particular attention to low income families and children. This is the only organization in the country that focuses exclusively on the complex legal issues surrounding the establishment and provision of child care. This site contains information about their current initiatives as well as what the state of child care is today, publications, a newsletter and legal updates, information about contracts and liability, and links to other sites that provide information about child, child care, child development principles, and legal advocacy on behalf of children. To contact the CCLC:

The Child Care Law Center
973 Market St.
Suite 550
San Francisco, CA 94103
Tel: (415) 495-5498
Fax: (415) 495-6734

Juvenile Justice Center. http://www.abanet.org/crimjust/juvjus/home.html

Part of the American Bar Association, this organization works to improve the juvenile justice system by providing education, technical assistance, and information to juvenile offenders and advocates. This website contains information about the Juvenile Justice Center, Juvenile Justice standards and articles, information about the Due Process Project, state and federal juvenile justice information, defender resources, judges resources, District Attorney resources, parents resources, information about juvenile death penalty, a listserv, and links to over 500 juvenile justice websites. To contact them:

American Bar Association
Juvenile Justice Center
740 15th Street, NW
Washington, DC 20005
Tel: (202) 662-1522
E-Mail: juvjus@abanet.org

Juvenile Justice Clearinghouse. http://www.fsu.edu/~crimdo/jjclearinghouse/about.html

This site is sponsored by the Juvenile Justice Role Model Development Project at Florida State University and Florida A & M University and is a one stop shopping website for juvenile justice information, programs for at risk youth, and employment opportunities within this field. The site can be searched by category and also contains links to state government agencies that deal with delinquent youth. To contact:

Stephanie Bush-Baskette
Program Director
Room 155C
Bellamy Building
School of Criminology and Criminal Justice
Florida State University
Tallahassee, FL 32306-2170
Tel: (850) 644-4299
Fax: (850) 644-9614

National Association of Counsel for Children. http://www.naccchildlaw.org

This is a non-profit organization made up of professionals dedicated to the protection of children in the legal system. The NACC provides training and education to attorneys and child advocates and advocates for improved public policy and legislation for children. This website contains information about membership, a member directory, a referral network, conferences and training seminars, policy agendas, publications including a children's law manual and the Children's Legal Right's Journal, links to other sites, and information about the organization. To contact the NACC write to:

National Association of Counsel for Children
1825 Marion Street
Suite 340
Denver, CO 80218
Tel: (888) 828-NACC
E-Mail: advocate@NACCchildlaw.org

National Center for Youth Law. http://www.youthlaw.org/
This is a private, non-profit agency that assists attorneys and child advocates address legal problems of poor children and families. The NCYL provides legal information, conducts training programs, and serves as co-counsel in some cases. The website contains information about current legislation affecting children, articles about children's issues such as juvenile justice and child welfare and adoption, recent NCYL newsletters, a foster care litigation docket, their annual report, and links to other related sites as well as links to state and federal government sites. To contact the NCYL write to:
National Center for Youth Law
114 Sansome Street
Suite 900
San Francisco, CA 94104
Tel: (415) 543-3307
E-Mail: info@youthlaw.org

National Court Appointed Special Advocate Association. http://www.nationalcasa.org
Developed by a Seattle judge interested in using trained community volunteers to speak for the best interests of these children in court, this organization provides leadership for Court Appointed Special Advocate (CASA) programs across the country, holds an annual conference, publishes a quarterly newsletter, and promotes CASA through public relations efforts. This site contains information about the organization and programs, information about volunteering, links to other CASA organizations, and links to related sites.

Chapter 7

CHILD CARE RESOURCES

The web sites listed in this section provide information about day care, early childhood education, or after-school child care. Some sites provide programming information, such as the California Early Childhood Mentor Program web site, and others provide research and reports such as the National Child Care Information Center. There are other web sites offering information about child care than are listed in this section, however, this collection of sites contains the major sources of child care information.

California Early Childhood Mentor Program. http://www.ecementor.org
Supported by Federal Child Care and Development Block Grant Quality Improvement Funds which are administered by Chabot College through a contract with the California Department of Education, Child Development Division, this is the largest mentoring program for child care professionals in the U.S., providing training and supervision for child care workers. Mentors provide guidance and practical help for less experienced child care workers. This site contains information about the program, a directory of training institutions, community resources, a special section for students, information about improving child care, how to become a mentor, a discussion forum, and links to related sites. To contact:
Chabot College
25555 Hesperian Blvd.
Hayward, CA 94545
Tel: (510) 786-6638
Fax: (510) 786-6022

CareGuide. http://www.careguide.net

Based in San Francisco and privately held, this company's initial funding was provided by Allen & Co., the New York-based, private investment bank. This site is the leading online resource for information about child and elder care and contains a database of over 90,000 child care centers throughout the country. Searches for child care centers, preschools, after school programs, and family care can be done by state. There is also a resources center with checklists and information about selecting child care, a bookstore, articles about child safety, featured articles on a variety of subjects, and links to important resources.

Center for the Child Care Workforce. http://www.ccw.org

Formerly the Child Care Employee Project, this is non-profit research, education, and advocacy organization committed to improving child care quality by organizing around the issues of better compensation and working conditions in the field of early care and education.

This site contains information on research and policy, the early childhood mentoring alliance, state by state update on the Worthy Wage Campaign, a list of resources, surveys and reports related to employment in the child care field, and special event information.

Center for the Improvement of Child Caring. http://www.ciccparenting.org

One of the country's largest and most influential parenting and parent education organizations, this non-profit organization provides research, education, and training in order to improve the overall quality of child rearing and child caring in the United States. This site contains information about parenting seminars, a directory of national and international licensing opportunities, an opportunity to ask Dr. Alvy, psychologist and founder of CICC, questions, instructors' workshops, a catalog of parenting books, and information about their programs. To contact:

Center for the Improvement of Child Caring
11331 Ventura Blvd., Suite 103
Studio City, CA 91604-3147
Tel: (818) 980-0903
Fax: (818) 753-1054

Child Care Action Campaign. http://www.childcareaction.org

This is a non-profit, membership organization dedicated to stimulating and supporting the development of policies and programs that will increase the availability of quality, affordable child care for the benefit of children, their families, and the economic well being of the nation. This site provides information and research about the needs of children and families, facts and figures, press releases, information for employees and employers on improving the workplace, community forums, action guides for parents and providers, and information on how to contribute. This organization also produces educational material and a newsletter and brochure.

Child Care Aware. http://childcareaware.org

Sponsored by the National Association of Child Care Resources and Referral Agencies, this website provides information about child care resources including referrals to agencies in your geographic area, a child care resource book, a child care primer for parents, a list of federal day care centers, child care expenses, and financial assistance and eligibility information. To contact child care aware call: 1 (800) 424-8246

Child Care Experts National Network. http://www.childcare-experts.org

This is a community-based child care resource and referral website and is a product of The Danville Group, Inc. This site contains databases of resources for families, researchers, and policy makers. There is information on the supply of childcare and the availability of subsidies, a directory of childcare experts, a directory of experts, information on how to become a child care expert, and a list of publications geared for parents as well as professionals.

Child Care Law Center. http://childcarelaw.org

This is a national, non-profit legal services organization that works to foster high quality, affordable child care, with particular attention to low income families and children. This is the only organization in the country that focuses exclusively on the complex legal issues surrounding the establishment and provision of child care. This site contains information about their current initiatives as well as what the state of child care is today, publications, a newsletter and legal updates, information about contracts and liability, and links to other sites that provide information about child, child care, child development principles, and legal advocacy on behalf of children. To contact the CCLC:

The Child Care Law Center
973 Market St.
Suite 550
San Francisco, CA 94103
Tel: (415) 495-5498
Fax: (415) 495-6734

Council for Professional Recognition. http://www.cdacouncil.org

This non-profit organization works to improve the professional status of early childhood workers and helps to meet the growing need for qualified child care staff. This website contains information about the council, council publications, information about the Army School-Age Credentialing Program, The National Head Start Fellowship Program, Reggio Children/USA (an Italian organization which promotes the Reggio approach to early childhood education by sponsoring study tours and other learning opportunities), and information about The Child Development Associate National Credentialing Program. This program (CDA) is designed to assess and credential early child care and education professional based on performance and is funded by the U.S. Department of Health and Human Services.

Day Care Providers. http://www.daycareproviders.com

This parent-focused site is a national daycare directory that was created to assist parents find quality childcare. This website contains a bookstore, newsletter for parents and providers, parent and provider resources, a day care checklist, information on listing a day care on their database, a message board, a missing children directory, and links to related sites. To contact:

Day Care Providers
P.O. Box 68
Colton, SD 57018
Tel: 1-8PROVIDERS
Fax: (605) 446-3168

Do I Know You? Who's Watching the Children? http://www.doiknow you.com

This site provides a resource of comprehensive checklists and questionnaires for anyone looking for a child care provider. It is also possible to do a background check on potential caregivers through this site. To contact:

Do I Know You/ Who's Watching the Children
50 Blair Rd.
Poultney, VT 05764
Tel: (802) 287-5571
Fax: (802) 287-5542
E-Mail: zap@together.net

Healthy Childcare: Health and Safety Ideas for the Young Child. http://www.healthychild.net

This is the website for the award winning bimonthly magazine, Healthy Childcare. This publication provides information on health, safety, medicines, staff health, health education activities, and illnesses and is edited by the American School Health Association's Council on Early Childhood Health Education and Services. Through this site you can access previous issues of the newsletter, subscribe to the newsletter, access the Head Start health and safety resource guide, and visit links to related sites.

International Nanny Association. http://www.nanny.org

This is a non-profit, educational organization that serves as a clearinghouse for information on the in-home child care industry and is made up of nannies, nanny referral agency owners and personnel, and individuals who support the in-home child care industry. This site contains information about the organization, press releases, information for families and nannies, a member directory, publications including recommended practices for nannies and for placement agencies, a sample family/ nanny agreement, information about their annual conference, a public service announcement video tape, and links to related sites. To contact:

International Nanny Association
Station House, Suite 438
900 Hadden Ave.
Collingswood, NJ 08108

Tel: (856) 858-0808
Fax: (856) 858-2519

KinderCam. http://www.kindercam.com
This website is sponsored by ParentNet, Inc. and provides information about KinderCam, a device that allows parents to monitor their children at a child care facility through the Internet. This site also contains a demonstration, a list of KinderCam equipped child care centers, and what others say about it.

Mind Your Business. http://www.mybinc.com
This company provides background investigation and information services for child care services, nanny agencies, and corporations. This site contains and overview of their services such as criminal records checks, credit history, motor vehicle reports, and social security number tracing to name a few. To contact:
Mind Your Business
P.O. Box 1390
Maplewood, NJ 07040
Tel: (888) 8MYBINC or (888) 869-2462
Fax: (978) 763-8286

National Association of Child Care Resource and Referral Agencies. http://www.naccrra.net
This non-profit organization is a national network of community-based child care resource and referral agencies that provides information to parents and professionals on child care issues. This website contains information about the organization, steps to finding child care, advocacy, learning opportunities online, professional opportunities, a request for proposals, publications, press releases, information about their policy symposium, how to become a member, current events, and a links to related sites. To contact the NACCRRA:
NACCRRA
1319 F. Street, NW
Suite 810
Washington, DC 20004-1106
Tel: (202) 393-5501
Fax: (202) 393-1109

National Association for Family Child Care. http://www.nafcc.org

This organization focuses on providing technical assistance to family child care associations. This assistance is provided through developing leadership and professionalism, addressing issues of diversity, and by promoting quality and professionalism through NAFCC's Family Child Care Accreditation. This website provides information about the organization, membership, accreditation, and what's new in child care. There is also a board of directors and staff listing, a call for program advertisers and resource sharing, and information about their biannual conferences. To contact them:

Nation Association for Family Child Care
525 SW 5th Street
Suite A
Des Moines, Iowa 50309-4501
Tel: (515) 282-8192
Fax: (515) 282-9117
E-Mail: mafcc@nafcc.org

National Child Care Association. http://www.nccanet.org

This is a non-profit, professional trade association that focuses on the needs of licensed, private childhood care and education programs. This website contains an issue alert, information on how to join, a list of member state associations, professional development opportunities, federal legislative updates, and lists of who to contact to find out about quality child care and business issues. From this site you can also access information from the National Early Childhood Program Accreditation.

To contact:
National Child Care Association
1016 Rosser St.
Conyers, GA 30012
Tel: (800) 543-7161

National Child Care Information Center. http://www.nccic.org

This organization is supported by the U.S. Department of Health and Human Services and serves to promote child care linkages and support services for children and families. This website provides a calendar of events, child care technical assistance, Internet links, links to other HHS sites, a list of national organizations, a extensive list of publications and other child care resources by subject, state profiles, and White House initiatives. There is also a database of child care related directories including a directory of national organizations, state child care regulatory offices, and state child care home pages. To contact the NCCIC:

    National Child Care Information Center
    243 Church Street, NW 2nd Floor
    Vienna, VA 22180
    Tel: (800) 6165-2242
    TTY: (800) 516-2242
    Fax: (800) 716-2242
    E-Mail: info@nccic.org

National Institute on Out-Of-School Time. http://www.wellesley.edu/ WCW/CRW/SAC/

Formerly the School-Age Child Care Project, this institute is sponsored by Wellesley Colleges' Center for Research on Women and was developed to improve the quality and quantity of school-age care programs nationally. This site contains news and announcements, a calendar of events, information about training, information about current projects and initiatives, information about the National Improvement and Accreditation System and about the Massachusetts School-Age Coalition, publications and data, and other on-line resources. To contact:

    National Institute on Out-of-School Time
    Center for Research on Women
    Wellesley College
    Wellesley, MA 02181
    Tel: (781) 283-2547

National Network for Child Care. http://www.nncc.org

Sponsored by the Cooperative Extension Program, NNCC works to unite the expertise and knowledge of child care of many of the nation's leading universities with parents, professionals, and the public. This site contains over 1000 publications and resources related to child care, support assistance from child care experts, a listserv, and a newsletter. To contact:

    Lesia Oesterreich

Tel: (515) 294-0363
E-Mail: nncc@exnet.iastate.edu

National Resource Center for Health and Safety in Child Care. http://nrc.uchsc.edu
This is funded by the U.S. Maternal and Child Health Bureau and located at the University of Colorado Health Sciences Center in Denver, CO. The NRC works to promote health and safety in out of home child care settings. This website provides licensure regulations for all 50 states and the District of Columbia as well as information on a host of child care subjects, links to other child care websites, documents such as the *National Health and Safety Performance Standards* and *Stepping Stones to Using Caring for Our Children*, as well as other child care information and resources. The NRC's mailing address is:

NRC for Health and Safety in Child Care
UCHSC School of Nursing
C-287
4200 E. 9th Avenue
Denver, CO 80262
Fax: (303) 315-5215
Tel. (800) 598- KIDS

National School-Age Care Alliance. http://www.nsaca.org
This is a non-profit, membership organization that works to support and improve after school programs for school-aged children by creating an alliance of professionals on the local and national level, develops and promotes national standards, offers professional development and networking, and helps form public policy. This website contains information about membership, NSACA accreditation, a list of NSACA accredited programs by state, conferences, professional development, public policy, their journal entitled *School Aged Review*, instructions for submitting a manuscript, and an opportunity to offer feedback. To contact NSACA:

The National School Age Care Alliance
1137 Washington Street
Boston, MA 02124
Tel: (617) 298-5012

Fax: (617) 298-5022
E-Mail: staff@nsaca.org

The SOHO Center. http://www.child2000.org

This organization is a non-profit national resource for quality child care and education and offers programs and services such as literacy training, a model school, child care related support services, child care training, and a resource library. The site contain information on the center's National Children's Literacy Initiative, information about the center, a national child care resource directory, a summary of the center's REACH Initiative to address child care needs, newsletters, recent grants they've received, a list of corporate sponsors, and links to related sites.

USA Child Care. http://www.usachildcare.org

This non-profit organization works to change policies that improve child care for low income and moderate income families. This website contains information about the organization, information about the Kidsrate Campaign, hot topics in child care, the National Development Project, a list of affiliates, and the USA Child Care Digest. To contact:

USA Child Care
3603 NE Basswood Dr.
Lee's Summit, MO 64064
Tel: (800) 484-9392
Fax: (816) 373-5914
E-Mail: usacc@usachildcare.org

Watch Me Grow. http://www.watch-me.com/wmgus.htm

This website is a division of the Odyssey Childcare and Development Company and is a service that allows parents to "see" their children's daytime activities over the Internet. This site contains information about Watch Me Grow, a sample of their service. A map of states currently using this technology, and the benefits of using Watch Me Grow. To contact:

Watch Me Grow
1720 130th Ave NE
Bellevue, WA 98005
Tel: (800) 483-5597

Fax: (425) 881-2737
E-Mail: mail@watchmegrow.com

White House Conference on Child Care. http://www.whitehouse.gov/WH/New/Childcare/index.html
This website offers information about the conference held on 10/23/99 which brought together parents, caregivers, business leaders and child care experts to explore how the public and private sectors can respond to the need for affordable and safe child care. This site includes President Clinton's remarks, regional satellite downlink sites, and other information about the conference.

Chapter 8

EDUCATION RESOURCES

This section contains an extensive list of web sites pertaining to the education of children. Perhaps the most useful site in this collection is the Educational Resources Information Center (ERIC) web site which is the primary resource for education information. There are also web sites that offer information about specific educational issues such as the National Association of Safe Schools web site which provides information about school safety, or the Sexuality Information and Education Council of the United States web site which offers information about school sex education programs.

American Library Association. http://www.ala.org
This organization provides leadership for the development, promotion, and the improvement of library and information services and the profession of librarianship in order to enhance learning and ensure access to information for all. This website contains information about library advocacy, education, ALA interests and activities, a directory of American libraries on line, an online store, library and research center facts sheets, a database of online periodicals, an archives maintained by the University of Illinois at Urbana-Champaign, key reference documents including policy manual, code of ethics and bylaws, links to library web resources, and a list of events and conferences. There is also a special section for kids.

Aspiring Youth. http://www.aspiringyouth.org/welcome.html
This non-profit organization works to help at risk youth succeed in school and life, with a focus on the middle school years when children are transitioning from childhood to adolescence. This site contains information about the organization, a calendar of events, an overview of their programs, child and youth development information, and links to related sites. To contact:

Aspiring Youth
6250 Westpark, Suite 217
Houston, TX 77057
Tel: (713) 334-3330
Fax: (713) 334-3366
E-Mail: Aspireyou@aol.com

The Center for Career Development in Early Childhood Education. http://ericps.ed.uiuc.edu/ccdece/ccdece.html
Sponsored by Wheelock College, the center was founded to improve the quality of early care and education for children by creating a viable career development system for early childhood practitioners; and promote the definition of early care and education both as a professional field and as a field of study. This website is a partner of the ERIC Clearinghouse on Elementary and Early Childhood Education and the University of Illinois at Urbana-Chamapign and provides an extensive list of links and Internet resources on the subject of early childhood education, a directory of publications and research reports that can be purchased, information seminars for administrators, and information about the center.

Children's Music Web. http://www.childrensmusic.org
This is a non-profit organization that is an on-line resource for parents and educators. This website offers reviews of children's music, information about music education, a radio list, an online newsletter, as well as special games for children. There are special sections for musicians and educators, links to related organizations, a list of corporate sponsors, reviews by popular musicians, and a public forum.

Comer School Development Program. http://info.med.yale.edu/comer
Produced by the Yale Child Study Center, the School Development Program is a systemic school reform strategy that is being implemented in more than 65 school districts throughout the country and funded by the Rockefeller Foundation with the goal of creating more holistic education. This site contains information about the program, an overview of the programs effects and evaluation, a list of publications, a newsletter, a list of Professional Development Centers, the national training schedule, and links to federal education websites.

Council of the Great City Schools. http://www.cgcs.org
This is a coalition of 57 of the country's largest urban public school systems and works to promote urban education through legislation, research, media relations, management, technology, and other special projects. This site contains a number of reports related to inner city education and management services for school administrators that can be purchased, national urban education goals, information about initiatives, data about the councils districts, legislative resources, a management resource library, employment services, and an opportunity to search the site for specific information. To contact:
Council of the Great City Schools
1301 Pennsylvania Ave., N.W. Suite 702
Washington, D.C. 20004
Tel: (202) 393-2427
Fax: (202) 393-2400

Developing Educational Standards. http://putnamvalleyschools.org/standards.html
Sponsored by the Putnam Valley School District, Putnam Valley, New York, this site provides a list of Internet sites with K-12 educational standards and curriculum frameworks documents. Standards are offered by state or by subject area. There is a comprehensive listing and links to clearinghouses and educational information from Canada and Papua New Guinea as well as links to popular publications that deal with education issues.

Early Childhood Education Linkage System. http://www.paaap.org/ecels/
This is part of the Pennsylvania Chapter of the American Academy of Pediatrics and provides health professional consultation, training, and technical assistance to improve early childhood programs in Pennsylvania. This site contains a number of documents related to health and early childhood education including a model of Child Care Health Policies, a fact sheet library, a special care plan for a child with behavioral problems, an audio and visual catalog, and links to related resources.

Ed Source. http://www.edsource.org
Based in California, Ed Source is an independent, nonpartisan nonprofit organization that specializes in clarifying complex education topics and policy choices - through balanced analyses of education issues and accurate education data. This website provides on-line access to data and information about education policy and finance issues. There are a number of publications that can be purchased through this site as well as information about conferences, new legislation, and links to related sites. To contact:
EdSource
4151 Middlefield Rd.
Suite 100
Palo Alto, CA 94303-4743
Tel: (650) 857-9604
Fax: (650) 857-9618
E-Mail: edsource@edsource.org

Educational Resources Information Center (ERIC). http://www.askeric.org
This is a federally funded national information system that provides access to an extensive body of education related resources. AskERIC is a question answering service for teachers, administrators, librarians, and others involved with education. The askEric site contains a list of all of ERIC's clearinghouses and links to them as well as a link to search the ERIC database. To contact ERIC:
ERIC Clearinghouse on Information and Technology
4-194 Center for Science and Technology
Syracuse, New York 13244-4100
Tel: (800) 464-9107
(315) 443-3640

Fax: (315) 443-5448
E-Mail: eric@ericir.syr.edu
URL: http://ericir.syr.edu/ithome

Even Start Family Literacy Program. http://www.goisd.k12.mi.us/GOISD/ EvenStart/main.html
Sponsored by Pennsylvania State University, this program is intended to improve the educational opportunities of Pennsylvania's children and adults by integrating early childhood education and adult education into a unified program and therefore focuses on the educational needs of the whole family. This website contains and overview of the program, eligibility requirements, program statistics, accomplishments, funding, and who to contact for more information.

Just Think. http://www.justthink.org
This organization works with students, teachers, parents, and the entertainment industry to promote literacy for the 21st century. This site contains information about the Just Think Foundation, information for teachers and parents, special sections for children, news and events, an online multimedia classroom, a lessonplan data base, student projects, teacher resources, employment opportunities, information on the body image project, and a photo gallery.

Merrow Report. http://www.pbs.org/merrow/
Produced by the Corporation for Public broadcasting, the Merrow Report is a quarterly documentary about children and education. This site contains program transcripts, a list of upcoming programs, an archive of past programs, video and audio messages of over 150 youth, resource listings, and a link to the PBS Homepage.

Montessori in the Home. http://www.saber.net/~mearth
This site provides resources to parents and homeschoolers including e-mail workshops, on-line consulting, chat rooms, newsletter, Montessori book store, Montessori and home school classifieds, publications such as *Basic Montessori: Learning Activities for Under* Fives, curriculum club, and sections just for kids. This site can also be viewed in French, German, Spanish, Portuguese, and Italian.

National Association for the Education of Young Children. http://www.naeyc.org

This is a national, non-profit, membership organization of early childhood professionals who work to improve the quality of education for children from birth through age eight. This website contains information about the organization, information for parents and professionals, public policy issues and news that affects young children, membership information, professional development resources, employment opportunities, information on their annual conference, a catalog of resources, and information about NAEYC's accreditation program.

National Association of Safe Schools. http://www.safeschools.org

Founded by a group of school security directors, this organization works to make schools a safe place for children by providing training, technical assistance, and publications to school districts interested in reducing school based crime and violence. This site contains information about their programs and services including training, school security assessments, and technical assistance such as reviewing school security policy and designing school security programs. There is also a list of publications, training schedules, and workshops. To contact:
National Association of Safe Schools
   P.O. Box 290
   Slanesville, WV 25445
   Tel: (888) 510-6500
   (304) 496-8100
   Fax: (304) 496-8105
   E-Mail: NASS@raven_villages.net

National Educational Service. http://www.nes.org

This is a non-profit organization serving families, educators, and communities by providing resources for those who work in schools as well as other agencies that serve children. This website contains information about NES, hot topics in child education, their newsletter, resources and materials including a catalog of more than 60 research-based books and staff development videos on effective discipline, school safety, multicultural awareness, drug abuse prevention, technology, and school improvement. Also included in this website is information on professional development, the NES bulletin board, and links to other related sites.

National Head Start Association. http://www.nhsa.org

This is a national, non-profit organization representing over 2,000 Head Start programs throughout the country and provides a national forum for the continued enhancement of Head Start services for poor children ages 0 to 5, and their families. This website contains information about Head Start, research and reports such as the 1999 poverty guidelines, a list of publications on a variety of subjects, information about legislative affairs, position papers, membership information, internship guidelines, virtual community services, and a list of Head Start partnerships. To contact Head Start:

National Head Start Association
1651 Prince St.
Alexandria, VA 22314
Tel: (703) 739-0875
Fax: (703) 739-0878
E-Mail: webmaster@nhsa.org

National Institute on Early Childhood Development and Education. http://www.ed.gov/offices/OERI/ECI

Part of the Office of Educational Research and Improvement of the U.S. Department of Education, this agency sponsors comprehensive and challenging research in order to help ensure that America's young children are successful in school and beyond, and to enhance their quality of life and that of their families. This website contains information about the agency, research and development, funding opportunities, publications, hot research topics, frequently asked questions, and links to related sites.

The National PTA. http://www.pta.org

This website is entitled Children First and is a one stop resource for information on the National PTA, the largest volunteer agency dedicated to promoting the education, health, and safety of children and families. Included in this site is information about the history of the PTA, the National PTA Archives housed at the National PTA Resource Center, a directory of state PTA organizations, a list of program sponsors and partners, a downloadable brochure, a photo archives, information on National PTA guidelines and fundraising, and other information. To contact:

National PTA Headquarters

330 N. Wabash Ave. Suite 2100
Chicago, IL 60611
Tel: (800) 307-4782
Fax: (312) 670-6783
E-Mail: info@pta.org

PACER Center. http://www.pacer.org
This is the Parent Advocacy Coalition for Educational Rights Center and is a non-profit organization that works to improve and expand opportunities that enhance the quality of life for children and young adults with physical, mental, emotional, and learning disabilities. This site contains publications, legislative information, projects and ideas, articles, new events, resources and links, and employment strategies for youth with disabilities.
To contact:
PACER Center
4826 Chicago Ave., South
Minneapolis, MN 55417-1098
Tel: (800) 53 PACER
(612) 827-2966
TDD (612) 827-7700

Pathways to School Improvement. http://www.ncrel.org/sdrs/pathwayg.htm
Produced by the North Central Regional Education Laboratory, this site contains information on professional development, parent involvement, leadership, assessment, technology, and at-risk youth. There are sections devoted to specific subjects, such as math, literacy, and science, information and resources on how to maintain drug-free schools, documents addressing the critical issues of integrated school services, resources and documents on parent and family school involvement, curriculum development resources as well as discussion groups and policy publications.

Problem Solver. http://www.problemsolver.org/welcome.htm
Produced by author/educator Eleanor Reynolds, M.A., this website is the electronic version of the *Problem* Solver newsletter. This newsletter is geared towards parents and professionals working with children and is filled with articles that teach adults how to use the problem-solving approach to children's behavior

and curriculum. Articles are focused on enriching children's learning environment, improving programs, enhancing curriculums, and answering questions. This website offers a special section for college professors, information about the author, and subscription information.

Reinventing Schools: The Technology is Now. http://www.nap.edu/reading room/books/techgap/welcome.html

Sponsored by the National Academies of Science and Engineering and the National Academy Press, this website contains a wide variety of information related to technology in schools. This site contains a large database of documents that can be downloaded, a search engine, ordering information, and access to an online catalog.

School Wise Press. http://www.schoolwisepress.com

A small, private publishing company based in California, the School Wise Press is interested in helping parents become more involved in schools by providing them with information and resources. This site contains publications, California school news, a legislative watch, and school profile reports used to compare schools across the country in a variety of areas including test scores, teachers' credentials, and students' ethnicity. The site also has a virtual library of information on issues of education and information about current legislation that affects education.

Sexuality Information and Education Council of the United States. http://www.siecus.org/home.html

This national, non-profit organization works to collect and disseminate information, and promote comprehensive education about sexuality. This site contains a list of publications, a school health education clearinghouse, a library and information services, a description of their programs, special sections for parents, teens, religious organizations, and policy makers, press releases, and reports and statistics on sex education.

Teaching Strategies. http://www.teachingstrategies.com

Founded by educator and author Diane Trister Dodge, this organization works to enhance the quality of early childhood programs by offering the highest quality curriculum materials, training programs, parenting resources, and staff development services that are practical, developmentally appropriate, responsive to the needs of the field, and reflect the most innovative thinking. This website contains information about what's new, a bookshop, an educator's page, online discussion lists, an online archive of resources, a parents page, links to related sites, and information about Teaching Strategies. To contact:

Teaching Strategies, Inc.
P.O. Box 42243
Washington, D.C. 20015
Tel: (800) 637-3652
Fax: (202) 364-7273
E-Mail: info@Teachingstrategies.com

Chapter 9

CHILD HEALTH RESOURCES

There are many web sites relating to child health. Some sites include information by major health care organizations, such as the American Academy of Pediatrics and the Institute for Child Health Policy. There are also sites providing information about health care, environmental health issues, birth defects, genetic diseases, physical activity, or international children's health. There are also sites that provide on-line medical journals and medical databases, such as the General Pediatrics web site.

Alpha Center. http://www.ac.org
This non-profit, non-partisan health policy organization works to help public and private sector clients respond to health care challenges by providing information, policy analysis, and planning and program management. This site contains a searchable database of newsletters, research and reports, updates on selected state health care policy developments, employment opportunities, information about national and state programs, and policy resources including links to relates sites. To contact:
Alpha Center
1350 Connecticut Ave., NW
Suite 1100
Washington, D.C. 20036
Tel: (202) 296-1818
Fax: (202) 296-1825

American Academy of Pediatrics. http://www.aap.org

This is a nonprofit organization of professionals that provides, advocacy, education, research, and services that improve pediatric care. This website has a wealth of information about public policy and children health care. There are monthly policy statements as well as practical information about children's health and safety, such as a shopping guide for car seats. Also available through the website is information about professional education, current research, publications, current press releases, membership information and an extensive list of agency contacts. To contact the AAP National Headquarters:

The Academy of Pediatrics
141 Northwest Point Boulevard
Elk Grove Village, IL 60007-1098
Tel: (847) 228-5005
Fax: (847) 228-5097

American Health Foundation. http://www.ahf.org

This is a non-profit research organization devoted to the prevention of chronic diseases with a special focus on cancer, and is a national resource for innovative approaches to nutritional and environmental health promotion programs. This site includes information about AHF, a list of faculty, publications and links, information about services, a directory of founders, members, and supporters, announcements, employment opportunities, and an opportunity to search AHF research database. There is also a link to the AHF's National Child Health Day site containing information about child health.

American Medical Association. http://www.ama-assn.org

This is one of the oldest and largest membership organization of physicians in the country and works to advocate for patients and physicians and promote and improve the medical profession. This site includes a Family Focus section and KidsHealth page that provide information on topics such as children's nutrition, safety and accident prevention, baby development, childhood infections, and emergencies and first aid. There is also the National Patient Safety Foundation, an on-line library, and on-line publication.

American Public Health Association. http://www.apha.org

This is the oldest and largest organization of public health professionals in the world and works to influence policies and set priorities in field of public health. This site contains a substantial amount of information about legislation and advocacy, public health resources, practice and policy as they relate to public health. There is also information about continuing education, membership, and affiliates and caucuses. To contact the APHA:

American Public Health Association
800 1st Street, NW
Washington, D.C. 20001-3710
Tel: (202) 777-2742
Fax: (202) 777-2534
E-Mail: comments@alsph.org

Best Fed. http://www.bestfed.com

This parent oriented website addresses the issues of pregnancy, childbirth, breastfeeding, babies, toddlers, education and parents. There is a database of breastfeeding articles that can be accessed through this site as well as an on-line bookstore, discussion groups, on-line magazines and newsletter, information about disciplining children, circumcision, diapering, child birth and unassisted birth, classifieds, a special section for dads, discussion groups, and parenting links.

Boys Town National Research Hospital. http://www.boystown.org

This well known hospital has a long history of offering help, hope and healing to abused, abandoned, neglected, handicapped or otherwise troubled children. They offer a host of pediatric services and is recognized as a leader in communication disorders research. This site contains information about the hospital and clinical services, information about current research programs, training, information about the admission process, special sections for parents and kids, and links to other sites related to communication disorders and professional organizations. To contact:

Boys Town National Research Hospital
555 North 30th St.
Omaha, NE 68131

Carnegie Corporation. http://www.carnegie.org

The Carnegie Corporation is a large philanthropic organization that offers funding and support to a large number of public service groups. This website contains a report entitled *Great Transitions: Preparing Adolescents for a New Century* which discusses the risks facing 10 to 14 year olds, gives recommendations for getting children started on a successful life course, and suggests actions that the community and institutions can take, particularly in the area of health care.

Center for Health Care Strategies. http://www.chcs.org

This is a non-profit organization affiliated with the Woodrow Wilson School of Public and International Affairs at Princeton University and works to provide technical assistance and information on issues related to managed care for low-income children and families. Two of their important initiatives are the Medicaid Managed Care Program and the Building Health Systems for People with Chronic Illness. This site contains information about these and other initiatives, several recent publications about health care, a resource center, and copies of their newsletter. To contact:

Center for Health Care Strategies
353 Nassau St.
Princeton, NJ 08540
Tel: (609) 279-0700
Fax: (609) 279-0956
E-Mail: mail@chcs.org

Children's Environmental Health Network. http://www.cehn.org

This organization is a national, multidisciplinary project dedicated to promoting the health of children as it relates to environmental hazards. The network is composed of experts in the fields of medicine, nursing, research and policy, who represent national child and health organizations. This site contains a resource guide on children's environmental health, information on education, policy, and research in the area of environmental health, and links to other sites. There is also a directory of employment opportunities, a directory of network members, a geographic focus index, a glossary of terms, and an organizational activity index. To contact:

Children's Environmental Health Network

5900 Hollis St., Suite R3
Emerville, CA 94608
Tel: (510) 597-1393
Fax: (510) 597-1399
E-Mail: cehn@cehn.org/webdesigner

Children's Health Indicators. http://www.ed.gov/pubs/YouthIndicators/ Health.html

From the U.S. Department of Education, this site contains a number of tables and graphs charting the number of children involved in a variety of health related issues, such as insurance, AIDS knowledge, physical fitness, violence, tobacco, alcohol, and drug use.

Children's Health Insurance Program. http://www.hcfa.gov/init/children. htm

This site is part of the Health Care Financing Administration and provides information and reports on Title XXI and the Children's Health Insurance Program. The site includes an outreach information clearinghouse, Title XXI legislation, and CHIP related White House and administration information.

The Commonwealth Fund. http://www.cmwf.org

This is a philanthropic foundation with four national program areas: improving health care, bettering the health of minority Americans, advancing the well-being of elderly people, and developing the capacities of children and young people. This website contains a publication list, information about current programs, surveys, fellowship information, an online newsletter, annual report, a number of reports on the state of Medicaid and other health concerns, and grant guidelines.

COSSMHO. http://www.cossmho.org

This is the Hispanic Health Link website and is a national and regional effort to provide Hispanic children with the best chance for a healthy and productive life through empowering Hispanic communities and families with the information, services, and access to public policy they need to improve the health and well being of their children. This site contains information about the organization, funding leads, information about initiatives and areas of interest, and reports including Healthy People 2010, which can be downloaded. There is also a list of publications, a newsletter, and videos.

Families USA. http://www.familiesusa.org/about.htm

This is a non-profit organization dedicated to the achievement of high-quality, affordable health care for all Americans. This site contains information about the organization and it's programs, a search engine to locate specific resources by subject, state by state health care information, a publication list, a listserv, news releases, information on child health expansion, a media center, links to managed care central, Medicaid clearinghouse, statistics and information on the uninsured, a national job bank, and other related sites. To contact Families USA:

1334 G St. NW
Washington, D.C. 20005
Tel: (202) 628-3030
Fax: (202) 347-2417
E-Mail: infor@familiesusa.org

Family Voices. http://www.familyvoices.org

This is a non-profit, non-partisan organization that supports families with children with special health care needs and advocates for the inclusion of a set of basic principles in every health care reform proposal. This website provides information about current news about health care for special needs children, information for parents, providers, and policy makers, a list of publications, fact sheets, resource information listed by state, information about Family Voices current projects, and information about how to join. To contact them:

Family Voices National Office
Post Office Box 769
Algodones, New Mexico 87001
Tel: (888) 835-5669
(505) 867-2368
Fax: (505) 867-6517
E-Mail: kidshealth@familyvoices.org

The First Years Last Forever. http://www.childrennow.org/health/ firstyears/index.html

This is the website for the Health Leaders' Forum on Early Childhood Development in collaboration with Kaiser Permanente developed for the purpose of examining how medical directors, health plan CEOs and senior leadership can promote the implementation and use of quality early childhood development services. This website contains information on children's health, family economics, health, as well as a media advisory, alerts, publications, and news releases. There is also a participant list of those participating in the forum and related fact sheets.

Focus on Child Health. http://www.hrsa.dhhs.gov/childhealth

From the World Resources Institute, this site provides information on the major causes of death for children around the world, improving children's health, industrialization and urbanization, and building a global consensus. There is also a list of state resources, information about their programs, an Insure Kids Now media kit, and a compendium of outreach models.

Food Research and Action Center. http://www.frac.org

This is a non-profit organization that works to improve public policy and end hunger and malnutrition in the United States. FRAC performs research on hunger and it's impact on low income families, reviews and analyzes how legislation and regulations affect food assistance programs, supports anti-hunger advocates, food banks, and other programs that help eradicate hunger, provides public information about hunger, and a clearinghouse of information about hunger and anti-hunger programs. This website contains information about FRAC, current news and analyses, information about federal food programs and hunger in the U.S., publications and products, and information about FRAC's Building Blocks Project and their campaign to end childhood hunger.

General Pediatrics. http://generalpediatrics.com

This site is supported by the Robert Wood Johnson foundation and managed by Donna M. D'Alessandro, M.D. and designed to provide pediatricians access to a wealth of information and a variety of subjects related to pediatrics. There are also links to Medical Image Search engines and to a number of pediatric, health sciences directories, policy statements and clinical practice guidelines, continuing medical education courses, professional societies, case studies and patient stimulations, and offers a large number of medical journals on line. This is a very comprehensive site.

Global ChildNet. http://edie.cprost.sfu.ca/genet/index/html

This site is sponsored by the Global ChildNet society and provides world wide networking for health professionals, child health workers, scientists, health planners, and other interested in child well-being. The site contains access to databases, information about what's new with child health, on-line conferences, and on-line issues of the *Global Child Health News and Review*. To contact:

GlobalNet
113-990 Beach Ave.
Vancouver, BC
Canada V6E 4M2
Tel: (604) 682-6008
Fax: (604) 682-6771
E-Mail: genet@unix.ubc.ca

Global Health Network. http://www.pitt.edu/HOME/GHNet/GHNet.html

This site is sponsored by the University of Pittsburgh and provides comprehensive resources in the areas that relate to public health. The information on the site is available in 6 languages in addition to English. Included on this site is a list of global resources and academic programs, links to related health networks, publications, grant opportunities in health related fields, and a newsletter.

Harvard Center for Children's Health. http://www.hsph.harvard.edu/children/

This organization is made up of over 100 Harvard Graduate School Professors and works to promote collaboration among researchers, policy makers, community providers and others to improve the health, development, and well-being of children. This site contains information about current Harvard research projects, the newsletter, a list of public events and links to related sites.

Child Health Resources

Health Care Financing Administration. http://www.hcfa.gov
This is the federal agency that administers the Medicare, Medicaid, and Child Health Insurance Programs. This site contains information and reports on these health care programs, information on projects and initiatives of the HCFA, statistics and data, research information, an information clearinghouse, laws and regulations, and links to other government sites.

Healthy Families. http://www.healthyfamilies.ca.gov/Default1.htm
This is a state and federal funded health coverage program for children with family incomes above the level eligible for Medicaid. This site contains information about the program, a handbook with an application to the program, and information about doctors that are part of the Healthy Families Program. To contact: E-Mail: www.mrmib.ca.gov

Inside Healthcare. http://www.insidehealthcare.com
Produced by Barry L. Hock, this is a comprehensive on-line directory of information on healthcare, policy, managed care, children and family health, education, training, research, ethics, health care law, Medicaid and Medicare, Nurses' Issues and much more. There are also links to Medline Plus, Duke University Health Policy Cyberexchange, Harvard's Countyway Web Catalog and several other on-line directories, information and resources on policy, the corporatization of health care, ethics, health care expenditure and financing, education, training, research, wellness and consumer resources, and much more. There are also lists of funding sources, health care organizations, and a health care humor section.

Institute for Child Health Policy. http://www.ichp.edu
This organization is a state-wide Institution of Florida's State University System and works to improve the health status of infants and children in both the state of Florida as well as the whole country by formulating and evaluating health policies, programs and systems. This site contains information about organization and financing of care for children and youth with special needs, child health systems in Florida, outreach and education, and research in organizing and financing health care. There are also links to reports available on-line. To contact:
Institute for Child Health Policy
5700 SW 34th Street, Suite 323

Gainesville, FL 32608-5367
Tel: (888) 433-1851

Kaiser Family Foundation. http://www.kff.org
This is an independent health care philanthropy that focuses on four main areas: health policy, reproductive health, HIV policy, and health and development in South Africa. This site contains information about these four subjects as well as state health facts, a link library, surveys, the Kaiser Commission of Medicaid and the Uninsured, and an on-line grant application. To contact:
Kaiser Family Foundation
2400 Sand Hill Rd.
Menlo Park, CA 94025
Tel: (650) 854-9400
Fax: (650) 854-4800

Kids Care. http://www.kidscare.net
This is an information network whose goal is to provide timely information concerning Medicaid prior authorization, guideline content and updates. This site contains a database of Children's Medical Services personnel and community based offices, public access information sites, and links to services.

KidsHealth. http://kidshealth.org
From the Nemours Foundation, a non-profit organization devoted to children's health, this website contains information on health care for professionals as well as children and parents. There are sections about speech disorders and teens, autism, severs combined immunodeficiency disorders, and a search engine to search the site for specific information. There is also a large database of information for parents on a variety of subjects and information about the Nemours Foundation.

Kidsource Online. http://www.kidsource.com
This family oriented website provides education and health care information for parents and professionals. There are specific sections for information on newborns, toddlers, preschoolers, K-12, a store, a list of organizations, guide to the best software, articles and forums on health and safety, what's new archives,

media information, recall notes, access to Internet safety software, a search engine, education articles, and media information.

March of Dimes. http://www.modimes.org
This national, non-profit organization works to improve the health of babies by preventing birth defects and infant mortality. This website can be viewed in both English and Spanish and provides infant health statistics, birth defects information, a resource center, employment opportunities, a health library, request for proposals, professional education, youth volunteer opportunities, employer based health programs, community programs, Folic Acid Campaign, links to state websites, links to congressional websites, advocacy updates, and facts sheets.

Medicaid Clearinghouse. http://www.familiesusa.org/medicaid
Part of the Families USA website, site provides information about the state and federal issues of Medicaid and children's health as well as the status of current legislation, resource information, and an opportunity to get involved through the Medicaid Advocacy Network.

MedWeb. http://www.MedWeb.Emory.Edu/MedWeb/default.htm
This site is sponsored by Emory University Health Sciences Center Library and is a directory of medical links to medical resources and a database of on-line information, reports and an extensive array of professional and academic journals. Searches can be performed by keyword or specific title.

National Center for Health Statistics. http://www.cdc.gov/nchs
This site is sponsored by the Center for Disease Control and Prevention and contains a large number of statistics on a variety of health related subjects. The site also offers links to other statistics websites, a data warehouse, surveys and data collection systems, publications and news releases.

National Health Law Program News and Headlines. http://healthlaw.org
This is a national public interest law firm that seeks to improve health care for America's working and unemployed poor, minorities, the elderly and people with disabilities. NHeLP serves legal services programs, community-based organizations, the private bar, providers and individuals. This website contains recent news articles published throughout the country on topics relating to health

policy and law such as child health, federal advocacy, racial and cultural issues, reproductive health, managed care, immigrant health and more. There is also an archive section to retrieve older articles and a listing of over 40 links to newspapers throughout the country, a database of job opportunities, information on training, litigation, research, and consulting services, and links to related sites.

National Library of Medicine. http://www.nlm.nih.gov

Located at the National Institutes of Health in Bethesda, Maryland, this is the world's largest medical library. This website contains health information, access to Medline and Medline plus, access to the library catalog, databases, publication, training, and grants, information about research programs, and information on current exhibits. To contact:

Donald A.B. Lindberg, M.D.
National Library of Medicine
8600 Rockville Pike
Bethesda, MD 20894
Tel: (888) FINDNLM

National Longitudinal Study of Adolescent Health. http://www.cpc.unc.edu /addhealth/

This is a study being performed by the Carolina Population Center at the University of North Carolina at Chapel Hill of the health related behaviors of Adolescents in grades 7-12. This site contains information about the study, data sets, codebooks, publications and presentations, and much more.

Office of Disease Prevention and Health Promotion. http://odphp.osophs. dhhs.gov/

This federal agency works in conjunction with the U.S. Department of Health and Human Services, Office of Public Health Science, and Office of the secretary to strengthen the disease prevention and health promotion priorities within the framework of the Department of Health and Human Services. This site contains on-line publications including the Guide to Clinical Preventive Services, the Prevention Report, and Healthy People 2010 Objectives, fact sheets, announcements of upcoming events, and links to other related sites.

Office of Health Policy. http://aspe.os.dhhs.gov/health/hphome.htm
Part of the Department of Health and Human Services, this agency is responsible for policy development– including policy planning and coordination, policy and budget analysis, review and formulation of legislation and regulations, and the conduct and coordination of research and evaluation on issues relating to health policy. This website offers on-line research on health policy and child health, funding information, information on children's health insurance issues, and a search engine to locate reports and publications by subject.

Pediatric Points of Interest. http://www.med.jhu.edu/peds/neonatology
This site is a searchable collection of links to resources in pediatrics and child health and is produced by the Department of Pediatrics at Johns Hopkins University. Links include hospitals, patient education material, journals, Medline database, organizations in pediatrics and medicine, and parenting resources.

PEDINFO. http://pedinfo.org
This site is an on-line index for pediatricians and others interested in child health. The site contains a wealth of information relating to child health and pediatrics, including topics such as child abuse, adoption, and school health. Resources are divided by clinical areas and subspecialties as well as by condition. There are also on-line journals, newsletters, links to professional organizations and hospitals, and access to health related software.

Physical Activity and Health: A Report of the Surgeon General. http://www.healthfinder.gov/text/docs/DOC0383.htm
This on-line report is provided by the Center for Disease Control and contains information about adolescents and physical activity and suggestions for what communities can do to promote physical activity.

Rare Genetic Diseases In Children. http://mcrc22.med.nyu.edu/murphp01/homenew.htm
This site is sponsored by New York University Medical Center and is a comprehensive directory of resources and information of rare genetic diseases in children. This site includes a resource directory, a message board, Internet search tools, and links to information on specific diseases. There is also a special section for kids with genetic diseases.

Sexuality Information and Education Council of the United States. http://www.siecus.org/home.html

This national, non-profit organization works to collect and disseminate information, and promote comprehensive education about sexuality. This site contains a list of publications, a school health education clearinghouse, a library and information services, a description of their programs, special sections for parents, teens, religious organizations, and policy makers, press releases, and reports and statistics on sex education.

State Children's Health Insurance Program. http://www.air-dc.org/cecp/resources/achip.html

This site is part of the Center for Child Health and Mental Health Policy at Georgetown University Child Development Center and works to improve the quality of life for children with special needs. This site provides a comprehensive look at the new State Children's Health Insurance Program as well as an annotated bibliography and links to SCHIP documents and research.

Texas Pediatric Surgical Associates. http://www.pedisurg.com

This is the website of the Texas Pediatric Surgical Associates at the University of Texas Medical School at Houston and contains a large amount of information on pediatric surgical conditions for both practitioners and families.

Youth Indicators 1993. http://www.ed.gov/pubs/YouthIndicators/index.html

This site contains information on the trends in well-being of American youth from the National Center for Education Statistics and the U.S. Department of Education. Categories are home, school, health, citizenship and values, and future.

World Health Organization. http://www.who.int

This international, non-profit organization works to help people worldwide attain the highest possible level of health. This site contains an overview of the WHO, information on a variety of health topics ranging from communicable diseases to health technology, information sources, reports including the World Health Report 2000 and disease outbreak news, WHO regional offices, related links, an opportunity to search the site for specific information, and links to other UN sites.

Chapter 10

CHILD SAFETY RESOURCES

This collection of web sites provides information relating to issues of child safety, such as child abuse and neglect, child injuries, and child violence. The National Clearinghouse on Child Abuse and Neglect Information is an excellent resource for documents and other information about the subject of abuse and neglect. The Injury Control Resource Information Network is a comprehensive resource for information and statistics about injuries and the Join Together web site is certainly worth exploring if information on gun violence is needed. This compilation of web sites offers extensive resources and information and should be helpful to anyone exploring these topics.

American Coalition for Abuse Awareness Newsletter. http://www.sover. net/~schwoof/newshead.html
This non-profit membership organization works to improve the quality of life for children and adult survivors of incest and sexual abuse, physical and emotional abuse through advancements in law, public policy, and the education of the public and professionals interested in the well-being of children. This site contains the electronic newsletter for the organization, which includes a conference calendar and links to other Internet resources. To contact:
American Coalition for Abuse Awareness
P.O. Box 27959
Washington, DC 20038-4688
Tel: (202) 462-4688
Fax: (202) 462-4689

American Professional Society on the Abuse of Children. http://www.apsac.org/

This is an interdisciplinary organization made up of professionals who are concerned with child maltreatment and provides a forum for discussing professional issues, encourages research, and provides information on current child maltreatment issues to professionals. This website provides information about the organization and state chapters, professional education, legislation, publications, memberships, public affairs, and how to make a donation.

Child Abuse Prevention Network. http://child.cornell.edu/capn.html

Sponsored by LifeNet, Inc. and Cornell University's Family Life Development Center, this site is the world wide nerve center for professional in the field of child abuse and neglect. This site contains direct links to the major resource of child abuse information, statistics, link to the National Data Archive on Child Abuse and Neglect, child abuse research, listservs to stay current on hot issues, and links to federal child abuse resources.

ChildHelp USA. http://www.childhelpusa.org

This non-profit organization is dedicated to meeting the physical, emotional, and spiritual needs of abused and neglected children focusing efforts and resources upon treatment, prevention, and research. This site contains information about child abuse, a national child abuse hotline, information on reporting child abuse, a list of nationwide facilities, statistics, resources, and referrals. To contact:

ChildHelp USA National Headquarters
15757 N. 78th St.
Scottsdale, AZ 85260
Tel: (602) 922-8212

Child Protection Clearinghouse at the Center for the Study of Social Policy. http://www.cssp.org/cpc.html

Supported by a grant from the Edna McConnell Clark Foundation, this organization is a made up of a group of private and public agencies working to strengthen families and improve child safety by disseminating information about state and local improvements to Child Protective Services and to promote reform of Child Protection Service systems. This site offers over 500 documents related

Child Safety. http://www.twbc.com/srnfront.html1#Top
Managed by Safe Ride News Publications, Inc., this website provides information for parents, safety advocates, and health professionals on child safety. The site contains information about protecting children in cars, school buses, and on bikes as well as a list of resource material that is available, links to related sites, a special section for teachers, and access to the Safe Ride News and the Willapa Bay Company newsletters.

Children and Violence- Prevention Program. http://cliving.org/KIDS VIOL/new_page_5.htm
This is a program developed by the Conscious Living Foundation that helps prevent violence in children by improving communication skills, teaching anger and stress management and other life skills. This site contains information about the program, kids and teens training materials, what's new, products and services, and an opportunity to search the site for specific information. To contact:
Janai Lowenstein, M.S.
Conscious Living Foundation
P.O. Box 9
Drain, OR 97435
Tel: (541) 836-2358
Fax: (541) 836-2358

Children's Institute International. http://childrensinstitute.org
This is a private, non-profit organization that serves to prevent and treat child abuse and neglect in Central and South Los Angeles County, California. This website provides information about their programs, an overview of the agency, child abuse and related links, information about violence and abuse in Los Angeles County, publications, and a list of training seminars offered. To contact them:
Children's Institute International
711 S. New Hampshire Ave.
Los Angeles, CA 9005
Tel: (213) 385-5100

Fax: (213) 393-1820 Or
Burton E. Green Center
Torrance, CA 90502
Tel: (310) 783-4677
Fax: (310) 783-4676

Children's Safety Network. http://www.edc.org/HHD/csn
This site is part of the National Injury and Violence Prevention Resource Center and provides information, publication, resources, and statistics relating to injury and violence prevention. There is also a special section on resources related to school and occupational safety. To contact:
CSN National Injury and Violence Prevention Resource Center
Education Development Center, Inc.
55 Chapel St.
Newton, MA 02458-1060
Tel: (617) 969-7101, ext. 2207
Fax: (617) 244-343

Family Resource Information, Education, & Network Development Services. http://www.frca.org/friends.htm
(FRIENDS) This is the National Resource Center for the Community-Based Family Resource Services program. As part of the Children's Bureau, FRIENDS works with the National Clearinghouse on Child Abuse and Neglect to prevent child abuse and provide support to families. The website provides a virtual resource center where organizations can access services and materials, factsheets, and have conversations with others about current issues. FRIENDS also provides Telephone Technical Assistance and On-Site Technical Assistance to help with evaluation, development of networks, marketing, and collaboration. FRIENDS contacts:
Sharon Sneed (312) 338-0900, ext.159
E-Mail: sharon.sneed@frca.org
Jack Denniston (800) 888-7970
E-Mail: jldenniston@intrex.net

Injury Control Resource Information Network. www.injurycontrol. com/icrin/

This website is sponsored by the Center for Injury Prevention and Control at the University of Pittsburgh and serves as a way to access on-line resources related to the field of injury research and control. The site contains a slide show of ICRIN's structure, content, and benefits and information from the site can be translated form English to Spanish. Information available includes injury data and statistics, publications, injury specific resources, an overview of recent research projects, grant opportunities, software and related research tools, and links to government and related sites.

International Society for the Prevention of Child Abuse and Neglect. http://ispcan.org

This is an interdisciplinary international organization of professional who work towards the prevention and treatment of child abuse, neglect, and exploitation globally. This site contains an overview of the organization, training events, a newsletter, membership information, and links to related sites. To contact:

International Society for the Prevention of Child Abuse and Neglect
200 N. Michigan Ave., Suite 500
Chicago, IL 60601
Tel: (312) 578-1401
Fax: (312) 578-1405
E-Mail: ISPCAN@AOL.com

Join Together Online: Gun Violence. http://www.jointogether.org/ gv/frontpage.jtml

A project of Boston University School of Public Health, this site disseminates resources and information to individuals, community activists, and professionals who are working to reduce firearm-related injuries and deaths. There is a wealth of information related to gun violence and extensive resources and links. There is also a large funding database with links to hundreds of funding resources. There are facts about gun violence and featured articles and top news stories. There is also public policy information, prevention curricula, and information on substance abuse and treatment programs. To contact:

Join Together

441 Stuart St.
Boston, MA 02116
Tel (617) 437-1500
Fax: (617) 437-9394
E-Mail: info@jointogether.org

Minnesota Center Against Violence and Abuse. ttp://www.mincava.umn.edu
Sponsored by the University of Minnesota, this is an electronic clearinghouse with access to thousands of Gopher servers, interactive discussion groups, newsgroups, and websites on the topic of violence and abuse. Documents can be downloaded. Topics that can be searched are education and training resources, web links on violence, papers and reports, funding resources, resources for professionals, art and poetry, call for materials, child abuse prevention statistics, and much more. To contact:
Minnesota Center Against Violence and Abuse
386 McNeal Hall
1985 Buford Ave.
University of Minnesota
Saint Paul, MN 55108
Tel: (612) 624-0721
Fax: (612) 625-4288
E-Mail: mincava@umn.edu

National Child Rights Alliance. http://home.att.net/~alexist/ncra/frames.htm
Founded by seven survivors of abuse, this is a nationwide movement of youth and adult survivors of child abuse and neglect that focuses on children's rights and improving social justice for all oppressed groups. This site contains a number of on-line documents related to child abuse and neglect that can be down loaded, the Youth Bill of Rights, The Freedom Voice newsletter, suggestions for how to help, and links to related sites. To contact:
National Child Rights Alliance
P.O. Box 61125
Durham, NC 27705
Tel: (919) 479-7130
E-Mail: JIMSENTER@delphi.com

National Children's Advocacy Center. http://www.ncac-hsv.org

This is a non-profit agency that provides prevention, intervention, and treatment services to physically and sexually abused children and their families. This website contains information about the NCAC, training seminars, publications, prevention and intervention of child abuse, and information about their video conferences as well as a call for papers. To contact the NCAC:

National Children's Advocacy Center
200 Westside Square
Suite 700
Huntsville, AL 35801
Tel: (256) 533-0531
Fax: (256) 534-6883
E-Mail: webmaster@ncac-hsv.org

National Center on Child Fatality Review. http://child.cornell.edu/ncfr/home.htm

This center is sponsored by the Interagency Council on Child Abuse and Neglect at Cornell University. The NCFR is made up of interdisciplinary teams that examine each case of child death to see the interplay between medical, criminal, and child protective concerns, and how communities can respond more effectively to prevent child deaths. This website contains a report on child deaths in California, a national directory of Child Fatality Review Teams, and more information about the Inter-Agency Council on Child Abuse and Neglect.

National Clearinghouse on Child Abuse and Neglect Information. http://www.calib.com/nccanch/prevmnth/index.htm

This website is supported by the Children's Bureau of the Department of Health and Human Services and is a resource for information on the prevention, identification, and treatment of child abuse and neglect and related child welfare issues. This website provides a documents database, a national organizations database, a prevention programs database, and a child abuse and neglect thesaurus. There is also a list and catalog of publications, information about services they provide, a calendar of events, funding information, and links to other related sites. To contact them:

National Clearinghouse on Child Abuse and Neglect Information
330 C Street, SW

Washington, DC 20447
Tel: (800) 394-336
(703) 385-7565
Fax: (703) 385-3206
E-Mail: nccanch@calib.com

National Committee to Prevent Child Abuse. http://bitcorp.net/UCPCA/

This is the website for the Utah chapter of the NCPCA. This site contains information about child abuse, legal issues, how to recognize and report child abuse, tips for parents, a list of resources, and contact information for the state of Utah.

National Crime Prevention Council. http://www.ncpc.org

Founded by FBI director Clarence Kelly and his assistant John Coleman, this organization works to prevent crime and build safer communities. This website is the organizations on-line resource center and provides information in English and Spanish. There is a special section for teens, facts about crime, publications, a calendar of events, information about local initiatives, program ideas, a public service campaign, training and tools, and an opportunity to search the site for specific information. To contact:

National Crime Prevention Council
1700 K Street, NW 2nd Floor
Washington, DC 20006-3817

National Data Archive on Child Abuse and Neglect. http://www.ndacan.cornell.edu

This site is sponsored by the Family Life Development Center, College of Human Ecology at Cornell University and provides research data relevant to the study of child abuse and neglect. This site contains datasets, publications, training institutes and workshops, discussion group for child maltreatment researchers, hot items, and other resources found on the Internet.

National Foundation for Abused and Neglected Children.
http://www.gangfreekids.com

This is a non-profit organization that is dedicated to improving the administration of juvenile justice in America and researches the incidence, cause, and prevention of child abuse and neglect. This site contains information about the organization, tips for kids, information about gangs, information about Shaken Baby Syndrome and child abuse, how to join, and missing children alerts. To contact:
NFANC
P.O. Box 608134
Chicago, IL 60660
E-Mail: gangfree@hotmail.com

National Resource Center on Child Maltreatment. http://www.gocwi.org/nrccm

This non-profit organization assists states and local agencies enhance their services to maltreated children and their families by providing training, technical assistance, consultation and written material related to prevention, identification, intervention, and treatment of child abuse and neglect. This website contains a list of board members, upcoming conferences, newsletters, publications, quarterly reports, and current workplans.

National Society for the Prevention of Cruelty to Children. http://www.nspcc.org

This is the United Kingdom's leading charity specializing in child protection and prevention of cruelty to children. This site contains and information bank of publications including publications, research and training material, research, and training materials, advice on child protection, job opportunities, a special section for children, a directory of supporters, and news and special events.

Pavnet. http://www.pavenet.org

This is the website for The Partnership Against Violence and is a virtual library of information about violence and youth-at-risk, representing data from seven different Federal agencies including U.S. Department of Education, USDA, HUD, HHS, and others. There is also a conference calendar, a user's guide, and funding information. To contact:

John Gladstone
Tel: (301) 504-5462
E-Mail: jgladst@nalusda.gov

Prevent Child Abuse America. http://www.childabuse.org/
Formerly the National Committee to Prevent Child Abuse, this organization works to prevent child abuse through training, information, and publications. This site contains information about the organization, links to state chapters and other related sites, child abuse facts, and tips for parents. To contact: E-Mail: ncpca@childabuse.org

Research and Training Center in Rehabilitation and Childhood Trauma. http://www.nemc.org/rehab/homepg.htm
Sponsored by the Department of Physical Medicine and Rehabilitation at the New England Medical Center, this organization works to conduct research about the causes, treatment, and outcomes of injuries to children, improve the delivery of services to children and families, and provide information to families and professionals working in hospitals, schools, and community settings. This site contains a newsletter, a bibliography, health care information for children, publications, research activities, and links to related sites. To contact: Research and Training Center in Rehabilitation and Childhood Trauma:

Department of Physical Medicine and Rehabilitation
New England Medical Center
750 Washington St., #75K-R
Boston, MA 02111-1901
Tel: (617) 636-5031
Fax: (617) 636-5513

Safe Kids. http://www.safekids.com
This is online resource of information for parents and those working with children about how to safely and intelligently guide children's use of the Internet. This site contains comprehensive information about privacy issues and the risks to children and teens using the Internet. There is information about Internet privacy issues, kids' rules for online safety, guidelines for parents, a family contract for safety, as well as articles, child safe search engines, and a directory

of parental control software. Safekids.com also offers the Safekids Newsletter that can be accessed through this website.

Willapa Bay Newsletter. http://www.twbc.com/wbcfront.html#Top
Produced by the Willapa Bay Company, Inc., this newsletter and website offers health education information geared to health educators, pregnancy education information for expectant mothers, and child passenger safety information for parents, advocates, and health professionals.

Chapter 11

Parenting, Adoption and Foster Care Resources

This section contains a wide range of web sites that include topics such as adoption, foster care, and family issues such as family preservation and divorce. A particularly good site for information about adoption is the National Adoption Information Clearinghouse web site. The Foster Care Connections site is a good resource about a wide range of foster care issues. Included in this section are also sites geared towards parents, such as the Single Parent Resource Center, which can offer information or interesting inks to other sites.

The Casey Family Program. http://www.casey.org
This is a private, non-profit organization that provides long term family based foster care, adoption services, guardianship, and family reunification services. This website provides information about the Casey Family Program, research projects, special projects and initiatives, links to other sites, and their annual report. To contact write to:
The Casey Family Program Corporate Headquarters
1400 Dexter Ave. North
Seattle, WA 98109
Tel: (206) 282-7300
Fax: (206) 282-3555

Child Support Information Site. http://www.supportfacts.com

This is an online service that provides information about child support. This website contains information on a variety of topics related to child support and two navigational tools to help you get around. There is a is also a comparison chart of what different types of agencies offer to those seeking child support and a list of sponsors who can be contacted to answer questions about child support.

Children and Family Research Center. http://cfrcwww.social.uiuc.edu

This is part of the School of Social Work at the University of Illinois at Urbana-Champaign and the Department of Children and Family Services. The CFRC was designed to coordinate public services and outreach efforts in the state of Illinois. The website contains information about current research and outcome reports, a list of grant opportunities and research proposals, the CFRC newsletter, upcoming events, and links to related sites. To contact the CFRC write to:

Children and Family Research Center
School of Social Work
1203 West Oregon St.
Urbana, IL 61801
Tel: (217) 333-5837
Fax: (217) 333-7629
E-Mail: cfrc@uiuc.edu

Children Awaiting Parents. http://www.ggw.org/cap/

This is an independent, non-profit organization that specializes in the adoption of special needs children and is also a co-sponsor of *Faces of Adoption: America's Waiting Children*, an electronic photolisting of special needs children awaiting adoption. This site contains information about the Adoption and Safe Families Act, a link to the special needs photolisting, information about being a foster parent, how to register a child, an adoptive parent survey, and links to related sites

Children of Separation and Divorce Center, Inc. http://www.bayside.net

This non-profit organization helps children and adults adjust to the process of separation, divorce, and remarriage by providing peer counseling services, community outreach and prevention programs, research efforts, and opportunities for professional development. This site contains list of publications, information about professional seminars, information about services they provide and information about their newsletter. To contact:

Children of Separation and Divorce Center, Inc.
2000 Century Plaza, Suite 121
Columbia, MD 21044
Tel: (410) 740-9553
Fax: (301) 596-1677
E-Mail: cosd2@juno.com

Children, Youth and Family Consortium. http://www.cyfc.umn.edu

Located at the University of Minnesota, this is an electronic clearinghouse of information and resources on the health, education, and well-being of children, youth and families. This website contains a table of contents, featured archives, experts file, a search engine to search the consortiums database, a list of CYFC publications, discussion groups, information about community partnership initiatives, news briefs, a staff directory, a newsletter, a parenting question-answer column, employment opportunities, and other web resources. To contact the CYFC:

Children, Youth and Family Consortium
University of Minnesota
201 Coffey Hall
1420 Eckles Ave.
St. Paul, MN 55108
Tel: (612) 626-1212
Fax: (612) 626-1210

Children's Rights Council. http://www.vix.com/crc/home.html

This national, non-profit organization works to assure children meaningful and continuing contact with both their parents and extended family regardless of their parents' marital status. This site contains information about state chapters, legislation, research on subjects such as the latest joint custody research, a catalog of resources, internship opportunities, results of the Best States to Raise Children in 1999 report, and links to related sites.

Faces of Adoption. http://www.adopt.org

Sponsored by the National Adoption Center and Children Awaiting Parents, two non-profit organizations, Faces of Adoption is an electronic resource that helps social workers and other professionals bring families together. This site contains a comprehensive adoption packet, a photolisting of children waiting to be adopted, a chat room to discuss issues of adoption, a list of books on the subject of adoption and links to related sites.

Family Preservation and Child Welfare Network. http://www.family preservation.com

From the South Carolina Department of Social Services, this website was designed with the goal of improving the quality of life for children and families by advocating information sharing to create positive change. The website contains information on child abuse and neglect, foster care, adoption, family violence, as well as federal child and family statistics. There is also a photolisting of waiting children and information on fetal abuse and childhood disabilities.

Family Resource Coalition of America. http://www.frca.org

Formerly the Family Resource Coalition of America, this non-profit organization works to help families and communities provide healthy environments for children. This site contains information about the organization, a list of resources and publications, a leadership roundtable, a downloadable self assessment tool kit, current initiatives listed by state, networking information, an on-line store, and special sections for family support issues and news. To contact:

Family Resource Coalition of America
20 N. Wacker Dr. Suite 1100
Chicago, IL 60606
Tel: (312) 338-0900
Fax: (312) 338-1522

Families and Work Institute. www.familiesandwork.org

This is a non-profit organization that addresses the changing nature of work and family life and is committed to research based strategies that foster supportive connections among workplaces, families, and communities. This site contains a call for papers, 1997 National Study of the Changing Workforce, publications such as *The Seven Lessons of Early Childhood Pubic Engagement*, community

mobilization forums, a list of funding resources, and *Ask the Children*, a study of what children think about working parents. There is also information about policy, work site research, evaluation and technical assistance. To contact:
Families and Work Institute
330 7th Ave. 14th Floor
New York, NY 10001
Tel: (212) 465-2044
Fax: (212) 465-8637

Foster Care Connections. http://www.geocities.com/Heartland/Acres/87961
This website is an index of resources on foster care and child welfare on the internet. Searches can be performed by categories including general links, regional listings, foster parent resources, journals, legislation, data, research, specific issues, child abuse prevention, and adoption.

The Foster Parent Pages. http://fostercare.org
This website is dedicated to foster parents and those interested in foster parenting and provides a large amount of information about foster parenting. There are articles and other sources of information about foster parenting, a chat room, a discussion area, books and reference material, information on addiction, legal references, a mentor program, and a section for foster children and foster parents can search for foster relatives they have lost contact with.

Healthy Families. www.freddiemacfoundation.org/html/founheal.htm
This site is sponsored by the Freddie Mac Foundation and coordinated by Prevent Child Abuse America and provides information for new parents up to five years after their children are born. The site provides information about their home visiting program which offers new parents education and parenting information, referrals to services and training seminars, and training and employment opportunities with the hope that this information will prevent child abuse and neglect.

National Adoption Information Clearinghouse. http://www.calib.com/naic/
This is a service of the Children's Bureau, Administration on Children, Youth and Families, Administration for Children and Families, and the Department of Health and Human Services and provides a wealth of information about adoption. This site contains on-line databases, on-line publications, information about funding, adoption statistics, introductory packages for prospective adoptive parents, a conference calendar, and links to related sites. There is also a list of NAIC publications including a guide to adoption sites on the Internet and an adoption library containing research reports and studies on all aspects of adoption. To contact the NAIC:

National Adoption Information Clearinghouse
330 C Street, SW
Washington, D.C. 20447
Tel: (888) 251-0075
(703) 352-3488
Fax: (703) 385-3206
E-Mail: naic@calib.com

National Family Preservation Network. http://www.nfpn.org
This is a national membership advocacy organization composed of public and private agencies that are involved with family preservation. This site contains membership information, a list of resources that can be purchased, what's new in family preservation, list of upcoming training sessions, a bulletin board, a bibliography, a newsletter, evaluations, and links to related sites. There is also information about their Intensive Family Preservation Services, a specialized, home-based service that teaches to families to enable them to stay together. To contact:

National Family Preservation Network
P.O. Box 2570
Laurel, MD 20709
Tel: (301) 498-0103
Fax: (301) 498-2909
E-Mail: info@nfpn.org

Permanency Planning for Children. http://www.pppncjfcj.org
This site is from the Permanency Planning for Children Department, a part of the National Council of Juvenile and Family Court Judges. As an organization, PPCD works to health judges make critical decisions of behalf of children. This site contains information about current projects such as the Expedited Adoptions project and the Child Victims Act Model Courts Project, technical assistance, publications, information about the organization, and links to other sites. To contact:
Permanency Planning for Children
P.O. Box 8970
Reno, NV 89507
Tel: (775) 327-5300
Fax: (775) 327-5306
E-Mail: ppp@pppncjfcj.org

Single Parent Resource Center. http://singleparentresources.com
This is a non-profit organization that is made up of single parents who are interested in helping other single parents by providing support and services. This website contains information about SPRC, a list of programs and services such as counseling, education, and financial services, a list of preferred vendors, links to single parent websites, career information, publications that can be purchased and downloaded, spirituality information, and supportive advice for single parents.

Stepfamily Association of America. http://www.stepfam.org
This is a national, non-profit, membership organization that provides information, education, advocacy, and research of and for stepfamilies. This website contains recent published articles, a catalog of publications and educational and resource material, information about step family advocacy, a list of programs and services, book reviews, training opportunities, stepfamily facts, a list of local chapters, and information on how to join. To contact:
Stepfamily Association of America, Inc.
650 J Street Suite 205
Lincoln, NE 68508
Tel: (800) 735-0329
Fax: (402) 477-8317
E-Mail: stepfamfs@aol.com

Survivors of the System: Foster Children United. http://www.azstarnet.com/ ~marier/sos/index1.html

This non-profit organization works to educate the public on the issues of foster care, promote services to assist foster care children, provide research and reports on foster care, and provide a voice for children in and from foster care families. This site contains current news and articles about foster care, a search engine for information and research on foster care, an art gallery, a foster parent forum, information about submitting documents, classifieds, a comedy corner, special sections for professionals and children, and a list of books related to foster care.

The Evan B. Donaldson Adoption Institute. http://www.adoptioninstitute.org

This website is geared towards adoption professionals and others interested in adoption research, policy, and practice and contains information related to the policies and practices of adoption, professional education, and research resources containing more than a 1,000 searchable abstracts. Also included are examples of adoption services, a staff directory, a list of advisory board members, a survey, publications that can be ordered, a newsletter, a newsroom, and information about relevant grant opportunities. To contact them:

The Evan B. Donaldson Adoption Institute
120 Wall St. 20th Floor
New York, NY 1000

Chapter 12

MEDIA RESOURCES

This section contains web sites that provide information about issues relating to children and the media. Topics include television and violence, media literacy, how health and social justice are depicted in the media, responsible media, how media influences children and adolescents, and children's use of electronic media.

About Face. http://www.about-face.org
This non-profit, volunteer organization is a media literacy organization that focuses on the impact the mass media has on the mental and emotional well being of women and girls. This site contains suggestions for how to change your community, a list of resources and links, visitor essays, art projects, discussion groups, tips and resources for parents and teachers, examples and ideas for personal change, facts, research studies, a directory of related organizations, and information on how to hold companies accountable including a gallery of offenders.

Ad Council. http://www.adcouncil.org
This is a private, non-profit organization, originally developed to rally support for the war effort during World War II, that uses advertising to stimulate action against the problems confronting Americans today, particularly those affecting children. This website contains information about current campaigns, a calendar of events, media materials that can be ordered, a community action network, information on how to create a campaign, information on the impact of

advertising, research including an issues tracking study, and other information about Public Service Announcements.

Association of America's Public Television Stations. http://apts.org/

This is a non-profit organization that supports noncommercial television. This site contains information and statistics about children, education and public television. There are also action alerts and information about APTS' legal and regulatory activities as well as a publications list (including a guide to technology) and links to related sites.

Center for Media Education. http://www.cme.org

This is an non-profit organization that works to improve the quality of electronic media on behalf of children and families. This site contains information about children's programming regulations, surveys on Internet marketing to kids and parents, a program to provide technical assistance to state-based organizations. It also includes a research initiative to understand the nature and scope of research on the use of interactive technologies by children, a section on democratic access which seeks equal access to new information technologies, press releases, and information about the Children's Online Privacy Protection Act.

Center for Media Literacy. http://www.medialit.org

This organization develops and distributes educational materials and programs that promote critical thinking about the media. This site contains teaching resources and trainings on media literacy, an email bulletin, a listserv discussion group from New Mexico State University, a resource catalog, information about media violence, a reading room, and links to other sites. To contact:

Center for Media Literacy
4727 Wiltshire Blvd
Suite 403
Los Angeles, CA 90010
Tel: (323) 931-4177
Fax: (323) 931-4474

Children and the Media Program. http://www.childrennow.org/media/media.index

This organization works to improve the quality of news and entertainment media both for children and about children's issues. This site contains a report on news media coverage of children's issues, as well as a number of resources about diversity in television including surveys of programs and their depiction of racial issues. There is also a publication list, an electronic newsletter, and links to other sites. To contact:

Children Now
1212 Broadway 5th Floor
Oakland, CA 94612
Tel: (510) 763-2444
Fax: (5100 763-1974
E-Mail: childrennow@childrennow.org

Children's Advertising Unit of the Better Business Bureau. http://www.bbb.org/advertising/childrensMonitor.html

This site provides extensive information about advertising as it concerns and affects children. There is a parents guide, self-regulatory guidelines for children's advertising, and a list of supporters, and business and academic advisors. The Children's Advertising Unit seeks to protect the interests of children in the media as well as on-line and they investigate misleading and inaccurate advertising claims in advertisers targeting children.

Children's Partnership. www.childrenspartnership.org/

This organization has published the Parents Guide to the Information Superhighway: Rules and Tools for Families Online. It is an on-line parents guide to the Internet and offers age appropriate guidelines for technology use by children and suggests ways to direct children towards positive and productive on-line experiences. You can access portions of it on this website.

Children's Television Workshop. http://www.ctw.org

This website contains information about CTW programs as well as special sections for children and parents, discussion groups and information on membership. There are also web pages for stories, activities, learning, printables, and many Sesame Street characters such as Elmo.

Corporation for Public Broadcasting. http://www.cpb.org

This organization is the largest single source for funding for public programming. This website includes a request for proposals, video and transcript information, minority consortia, scholarship information, information on PBS and NPR, and information about grants.

Girls, Inc. http://www.girlsinc.org/programs/recast.html

This site contains the Girls Re-cast TV Action Kit which is geared towards children and provides information to help girls evaluate TV programs' depiction of women and families. This includes a "reality check" quiz for girls to compare what they see on TV to their lives. The site also includes research (on topics such as girls and smoking), advocacy, the Girls Bill of Rights, tips for parents and other adults, and the Girls' Bill of Rights.

KidsNet. http://www.kidsnet.org

This is a monthly media guide that describes upcoming programs on television for children, families, and educators, referenced by air date, grade levels, and other topics. This site also has study guides for educators, parents, and other professionals working with children to be used as companion to the television program. Study guides are designed to accompany television programs and include topics such as black history month, Sherlock Holmes, and Israel to name a few. To contact:
KIDSNET
6856 Eastern Ave., NW
Suite 208
Washington, D.C. 20012
Fax: (202) 882-7315
E-Mail: kidsnet@kidsnet.org

Media Forum. http://www.cyfc.umn.edu/Media/index.html

This site is an electronic resource collection and networking tool and offers research, policy information, and opinion documents about how the media influences the lives of children. There is also an electronic bulletin board, links to other sites, statistics and surveys (such as the Student Media Survey and the Youth and Reading Survey), and a list of conference proceedings.

Media Literacy On-line Project. http://interact.uoregon.edu/MediaLit/ HomePage

From the University of Oregon College of Education, this site provides and extensive list of resources on media literacy, cultural studies, children and the media, as well as teaching resources including lesson plans and instructional materials. There is also a parent's corner and an opportunity to search the site for specific information.

Media Research Center. http://www.mediaresearch.org

This non-profit organization works to bring political balance to the nation's new media and responsibility to the entertainment media. On this site can be found the Parents TV Council (see below) which helps parents make decisions about viewing discretion.

Mediascope. http://www.mediascope.org

This is a non-profit policy organization that works to promote constructive depictions of health and social justice in the media, particularly as they relate to children and adolescents. This site contains services and resources for parents, entertainment industry professionals, journalists, researchers, and policy activists such as a number of recent publications, information on media ratings, academic research on topics relating to social and health issues in the media, a national television violence study, and access to the media policy clearinghouse which contains a wealth of information relating to children and the media. You are able to search their library by topic from a large selection of topics from advertising to violence. To contact:

Mediascope
12711 Ventura Blvd
Studio City, CA 91604
Tel: (818) 508-2080
Fax: (8181) 508-2088
E-Mail: facts@mediascope.org

Parents Television Council. http://www.parentstv.org

This non-profit organization provides information about trends in prime time television and family. The PTC publishes and annual Family Guide to Prime Time Television as well as many special reports throughout the year. The most recent report available on the site presents statistics of violence and sexual references in prime time from 1989 to 1999, it also breaks these statistics down by network. This website contains information about the organization, information on how to join their campaign, what's new in Hollywood, a partial list of the PTC press coverage, a list of television programs that receive their seal of approval, information about their celebrity advisory board, and links to family websites.

Public Broadcasting Service. http://www.pbs.org

This site includes resources for teachers, adult learning, a special section for kids, an on-line news hour, science and technology pages, and a list of PBS television programs (from Arts to Travel) and stations. It also includes information on the PBS Program for Democracy a sort of voter education guide.

Television and Violence. http://www.ksu.edu/humec/tele.htm

This smaller website sponsored by Dr. John P. Murray at Kansas State University, and contains a number of articles on television and violence from sources such as Hofstra Law Review and the Kansas Journal of Law and Public Policy, as well as links to related sites.

Chapter 13

CAMPING ORGANIZATIONS

Overnight and day camps are an increasing activity for children, especially during the summer. This list of web sites consists of some of the nations most important resources for information on children's camps. These sites contain information about programs for kids as well as camp regulations and several sites have direct links to camps throughout the country.

American Camping Association. http://www.acacamps.org
This organization is a community of camp professionals who work to enrich the lives of children through the camp experience. This website contains information about the organization, information on how to become a member, an interactive camp database, information and resources for camp staff, media resources, and a special section for parents. There is also a link to accreditation and standards information. They also include research on childrens' camps such as results of the National Inclusive Camp Practices study and the National Camp Evaluation Project. To contact:
American Camping Association
5000 State Rd. 67 North
Martinsville, IN 46151-8456
Tel: (765) 342-8456
Fax: (765) 342-2065

Association of Jewish Sponsored Camps. http://www.jewishcamps.org

This organization represents 33 non-profit camps for children and adults and provides information and referrals on their member camps. This website contains camp descriptions, a special section for camps for special needs children, information for staff, and a checklist of important information to ask when choosing a camp. To contact:

The Association of Jewish Sponsored Camps
130 East 59th Street
New York, NY 10022
Tel: (212) 751-0477
Fax: (212) 755-9183
E-Mail: info@jewishcamps.org

Boy Scouts of America. http://www.bsa.scouting.org

This is the official website for the National Council of the Boy Scouts of America which supports more than 300 local councils. This website contains information about the Boy Scouts, news and press releases, special sections for kids, a search engine to locate local councils, the annual report, information about camping facilities and the international camp staff program, magazines and publications, as well a host of other information about the Boy Scouts. It also contains information about the 6/28/00 Supreme Court decision regarding the Boy Scouts and homosexuality.

Girl Scouts of the USA. http://www.gsusa.org

This is the official website of the Girl Scouts of the USA and provides a wealth of information about the organizations, it's programs and services (which are quite extensive), educational and volunteer opportunities, newsletter, and links to local councils and camps. You can also access Girl Scout publications such as their annual report. There is a section just for girls as well as information geared towards scout leaders and volunteers and web resources.

National 4-H. http://www.4h-usa.org

This is the website for the 4-H national headquarters and contains information about the organization, a list of activities and events, resources (which include statistics and information on low cost kids health insurance programs), and a section just for kids, and links to 4-H partners, such as the USDA. There is also a 4-H search engine, links to state and international chapters, which provide information about 4-H camping programs. An extensive list of available curriculums with descriptions are also available on, for example, empowering kids online, wetlands and science and agriculture.

National Association of Therapeutic Wilderness Camps. http://www.natwc. org

This non-profit organization represents nearly 50 therapeutic wilderness camps that help troubled youth change the way they deal with their parents, schools, and other authorities. This website contains information about the NATWC, membership information, news, a schedule of upcoming conferences, a camp evaluation checklist (with questions to ask of camps such as who licenses them and how long they have been in operation), and a map of the US with locations and descriptions of the camps. To contact:
National Association of Therapeutic Wilderness Camps
4270 Hambrick Way
Stone Mountain, GA 30083
Tel: (404) 508-1036
Fax: (404) 508-1514
E-Mail: info@natwc.org

National Camp Association, Inc. http://www.summercamp.org

This organization is an independent, professional organization and is the recognized authority on summer camps for children. They provide online information and referrals for overnight camping. This site contains a camp advisory service, a camp chat room, additional camping resources, camp news, information about camp directors and a free on-line staff placement service. To contact call 1(800) 966 CAMP

YMCA Young Men's Christian Association. http://ymca.net

This is the website for the YMCA of the USA. This site contains information about the organization, links to local YMCA websites, information about lodging, special sections for kids, families, and communities, child care information, and a special section about YMCA camps. This camping section offers a list of YMCA youth and teen day camps throughout the country. To contact:
YMCA of the USA

101 North Wacker Drive
Chicago, IL 60606
Tel: (312) 977-0031
Fax: (312) 977-9063

YWCA Young Women's Christian Association. http://www.ywca.org
This is the website for the national YWCA. This site contains a brief history of the YWCA and what its purpose is. There are also links to local YWCA chapters, which provide information about day camps and other programs, a calendar of events, news, and ideas for how to get involved. To contact:
YWCA of the USA 726 Broadway, 5th Floor
New York, NY 10003-9595
Tel: (212) 614-2700
Fax: (212) 677-9716

Chapter 14

RELIGIOUS ORGANIZATIONS

Researching religious activities can be rigorous, since every faith and denomination has its own organization and associations, tenets, beliefs, practices, and policies. They differ widely with respect to their policies on children. The list of providing each would be beyond the scope of his handbook. However, there are some major web sites of religious organizations that are working to improve child well-being. These well-known sites provide primarily program information and may be helpful in assessing what is currently being done by the religious community to help improve the status of children.

Catholic Charities. http://www.catholiccharitiesusa.org
This is the largest private network of social service organizations in the United States and works to support families, reduce poverty, and build communities. This site contains information about the organization, an overview of programs and initiatives such as the Medicaid Outreach Initiative, Pregnancy, Parenting, and Adoption Services, and Residential Care and Services for Children. There is also a news media section, publications and videos, and a list of local charities. To contact:
Catholic Charities USA
1731 King St. #200
Alexandria, VA 22314
Tel: (703) 549-1390
Fax: (703) 549-1656

Congregations Concerned for Children. http://center.hamline.edu/spacc/ccc.htm

This is a non-profit organization that organizes the religious community to work to meet the needs of children, specifically focusing on children experiencing poverty or violence. This website contains information about CCC's mission and efforts to improve conditions for children. These include resources and training workshops to facilitate congregations becoming more involved in child advocacy. To contact the CCC:

Congregations Concerned for Children
Peg Wangensteen, Director
1671 Summit Ave.
Saint Paul, MN 55105-1884
Tel: (612) 646-8805, ext. 20
Fax: (612) 646-6866

The Interfaith Alliance. http://www.tialliance.org

This religious organization works to promote the positive role of religion as a healing and constructive force in public life. This site contains information on the organization, issues of the newsletter containing articles on a wide variety of subjects (such as curbing gun violence), a list of resources, and information about their activities such as strengthening public schools and promoting good government. To contact:

The Interfaith Alliance
1012 14th St., NW
Suite 700
Washington, D.C. 20005
Tel: (202) 639-6370
Fax: (202) 639-6375

Jewish Board of Family and Children's Services. http://www.jbfcs.org

This organization was established over 100 years ago and is one of the nation's largest and most respected non-profit mental health and social service agencies. Services are focused on the New York City area and include clinics, community-based programs, residential facilities, and day treatment centers. This website has information about their programs and services and information about their post-graduate training opportunities in early childhood, and an opportunity to search the site for specific information such as family violence, child bereavement, and ADD.

The Salvation Army. http://www.salvationarmy.org
This is a worldwide Christian church dedicated to meeting the spiritual, physical, and emotional needs of all people. This site contains a way to search countries worldwide to find out about Salvation Army programs and services. These include a missing persons bureau, information about their medical and social services such as children's homes, day cares, fresh air camps, domestic and trade schools, counseling services, probation homes, and alcohol and drug rehabilitation centers. There are also on-line resources that include articles and publications, Salvation Army documents, a clip art gallery, and webmaster resources.

Unitarian Universalist Association. http://www.uua.org
This is the national association for members of the Unitarian Universalist churches. The association has a large Children's Program that include materials and resources for anyone who wants to help children. They have a series of pro-child policies, including polices in child abuse, use of volunteers, child safety procedures, and other resources.

Chapter 15

SPECIAL INTEREST GROUP RESOURCES

There are many web sites that focus on information that may be of interest to specific populations. This eclectic section provides the location of some major special interest sites.

Adolescent Directory On-Line. http://education.indiana.edu/cas/adol/adol.html
This is an electronic guide to on-line information about issues affecting adolescents offered by the Center for Adolescent Studies at Indiana University. This website provides information about conflict and violence (such as peer mediation programs), mental health issues (such as ADD and depression), health and health risk issues (such as obesity and HIV), counselor resources, games, penpal information, sports info, and homework help for teens.

Advocates for Youth. http://www.advocatesforyouth.org/
This non-profit organization provides a number of services and programs for youth ranging from HIV education, teen pregnancy prevention and media protection to monitoring legislation pertinent to youth and provides a support center for school based health care centers. This website contains information on their various programs as well as press releases, job opportunities, and a resource site with their recent publications. To contact Advocates for Youth write to:
Advocates for Youth
1025 Vermont Ave., NW
Suite 200

Washington, DC 20005
Tel: (202) 347-5700
Fax: (202) 347-2263

African American Resources. http://www.rain.org/~kmw/aa.html
This website is a comprehensive directory of internet links and other information related to African American history and culture. Links include art galleries, civil rights museum, Association of Nigerians Abroad, the Endowment for Youth Committee, various minority institutions, NAACP, Boys and Girls Club, the Science Institute, Howard University, University of Virginia Library Web, and many more.

America Links Up. http://www.americalinksup.org
This is an online service that provides education about issues affecting children and is sponsored by a coalition of non-profit organizations, education groups, and corporations. This website contains information for kids and parents, information about ALU initiatives, online town meetings, information on area events, discussion groups, and online safety tips for parents and kids. It also offers general tips on using the Internet for parents and kids.

America's Promise, The Alliance for Youth. http://www.americas promise.org
Developed by General Colin Powell, this organization works to organize and mobile organizations serving children and youth. The website contains their 2000 report on the state of the nation's children, current news and events, and information on how to get involved with America's Promise. Searches on topics such as getting involved and community progress are based on geographic location. To contact them:
America's Promise
909 North Washington Street
Suite 400
Alexandria, VA 22314-1556
Tel. (703) 684-4500
Fax: (703) 535-3900
E-Mail: webmaster@americaspromise.org

American Red Cross. http://www.redcross.org/youth
The Red Cross provides a number of services such as disaster services, biomedical services, and armed forces emergency services, health and safety services, international services, and nursing. Specifically for children, the Red Cross provides babysitting training courses, caregiving information, and a number of training courses for youth to get them involved with volunteering. To contact the Red Cross write to:
American Red Cross
Attn: Public Inquiry Office
11th Floor
1621 N. Kent Street
Arlington, VA 22209
Tel: (703) 248-4222

Campaign for Our Children. http://www.cfoc.org
This organization is a joint effort of public and private agencies who work to provide advocacy and education on issues affecting children and teenagers. This site contains useful information on programs and advocacy campaigns aimed at improving the welfare of America's children. There is a teen guide, a parent resource section, technical support, teacher resources, a press room, a catalog of publications, facts and statistics, and a special section addressing teen pregnancy.

The Chapel Hill Training-Outreach Project, Inc. http://www.chtop.com/programs.htm
This is a non-profit organization that works to help poor, disabled, and abused or neglected children, specifically in North Carolina. The website contains information about Headstart, including the Code of Federal Regulations, respite information, information, resources and education for families, and assessment products and products for disability services. It also includes FRIENDS, Family Resource Information and Network Development Services that provides online access to resources of CHTOP as well as Family Support America in Illinois. To contact them, write to:
CHTOP, Inc.
800 Eastowne Drive
Suite 105
Chapel Hill, North Carolina, 27514

Tel: (919) 490-5577
E-Mail: mathers@intrex.net

Child and Family News. http://www.tufts.edu/cfn
A news service for journalists based at Tufts University's Department of Child Development. This site contains and info bank containing a wealth of information about issues such as violence, health, education, family, and poverty as they relate to children. There is also a section called Story Starters with examples of stories that can be composed with the site's information and an invitation for teachers and parents to submit a story. To contact:
Child and Family News
Eliot-Pearson Department of Child Development
Tufts University
Medford, MA 02155
Tel: (617) 627-5314
E-Mail: cfn@tufts.edu

Child Welfare Institute. http://www.gocwi.org
This organization is a national leader in the provision of child welfare training and organizational development consultation services to state and local government agencies and private agencies. This site contains information about the organization, highlights from their newsletter, information about the training program, a publications catalog, a list of upcoming events and links to other sites. There is also a link to the National Resource Center on Child Maltreatment, which is operated by the Child Welfare Institute.

Children and Family Research Center. http://cfrcwww.social.uiuc.edu
This is part of the School of Social Work at the University of Illinois at Urbana-Champaign and the Department of Children and Family Services. The CFRC was designed to coordinate public services and outreach efforts in the state of Illinois. The website contains information about current research and outcome reports, a list of grant opportunities and research proposals, the CFRC newsletter, upcoming events, and links to related sites. The CFRC emphasizes the integration of research and practice and has information and guidelines on the site for this purpose. To contact the CFRC write to:
Children and Family Research Center

School of Social Work
1203 West Oregon St.
Urbana, IL 61801
Tel: (217) 333-5837
Fax: (217) 333-7629
E-Mail: cfrc@uiuc.edu

Children of Alcoholics Foundation. http://www.coaf.org
This is a non-profit organization that works to help young and adult children of alcoholics and other substance abusers to break the cycle of addiction in families. This site contains information about the impact of parental substance abuse, information on training sessions, public service announcements, links to related sites, special sections for youth and college students, publications, and a special section for professionals. It also shares current research findings and answers frequently asked questions about alcoholism and families. To contact:
Children of Alcoholics Foundation
164 West 74th Street
New York, NY 10023
Tel: (212) 595-5810 x7760
Fax: (212) 595-2553
E-Mail: coaf@phoenixhouse.org

Children, Youth and Family Consortium. http://www.cyfc.umn.edu
Located at the University of Minnesota, this is an electronic clearinghouse of information and resources on the health, education, and well being of children, youth and families. This website contains a table of contents (from adolescents to youth and disabilities), featured archives, experts file, a way for visitors to search the consortiums database, a list of CYFC publications, discussion groups, and other web resources. To contact the CYFC:
Children, Youth and Family Consortium
University of Minnesota
201 Coffey Hall
1420 Eckles Ave.
St. Paul, MN 55108
Tel: (612) 626-1212
Fax: (612) 626-1210

Children, Youth and Families Education and Research Network (CYFERNet). http://www.cyfernet.mes.umn.edu/

This is part of the Cooperative Extension Services and sponsored by the National Children and Families at Risk Initiative and works to provide information about child and family issues. The website is called CYFERNet and provides a wealth of information for kids, parents and professionals about childcare (including nutrition, child development and inmmunizations), health, and family resiliency, literacy in science and technology, and collaborations with other organizations. This site also contains research reports, funding sources, statistics and demographics, evaluation tools, bibliographies, descriptions of successful programs, on-line activities for children, professional development training programs, and links to other related websites. To contact the CYFERNet team write to:

    Trudy Dunham
    CYFERNet Coordinating Team
    Minnesota Extension Service
    340 Coffey Hall
    1420 Eckles Ave.
    University of Minnesota
    St. Paul, MN 55108
    Tel: (612) 624-2247
    E-Mail: cyf@reeusda.gov

Children's Defense Fund. http://www.childrensdefense.org

This is a non-profit, private organization that works to serve the needs of children through advocacy, research, and support for child welfare agencies. This website contains information about children's issues, the Black Community Crusade for Children, news and reports on children, a list of publications including A Parents Guide to Child Support, and the CDF Book Nook. To contact the CDF national headquarters:

    Children's Defense Fund
    25 E Street NW Washington, DC 20001
    Tel: (202) 628-8787
    E-Mail: cdinfo@childrensdefense.org

The Children's Foundation. http://childrensfoundation.net
This is a non-profit organization that provides advocacy for caregivers, children and their families as well as research, information, and training on topics such as child care, health care, leadership development, child support, and welfare to work programs. This website contains information about the foundation, the National Child Support Program, the National Child Care Advocacy Program, CF research, CF publications, and a list of Internet resources. To contact the CF:
The Children's Foundation
725 Fifteenth St. NW
Suite 505
Washington, DC 20005-2109
Tel: (202) 347-3300
Fax: (202) 347-3382
E-Mail: info@childrensfoundation.net

Coalition for Asian-American Children and Families. http://www.cacf.org
This is a private, non-profit organization that advocates for Asian-American children and families and works to help health and human service providers address the changing needs of the Asian-American community. This website provides information about issues affecting Asian-American children and families and a comprehensive directory for Asian-American children and families. There is also a list of myths and facts about Asian-Americans, issues of their quarterly newsletter, membership information, statistics, a list of funders, a new Asian Kids InfoLink, and links to other websites.

Colorado Children's Campaign. http://www.coloradokids.org
This organization works to mobilize individuals and organizations to act on behalf of children, with particular attention to health, education, and safety of those most at risk. This site contains information about their current initiatives, including the Doll Project, a quality child care tax check off list, special sections for children, and information about corporations effect on children. A list of sponsors is also included on the site. To contact:
Colorado's Children's Campaign
225 East 16th Ave.
Suite B-300
Denver, CO 80203-1607

Tel: (303) 839-1580
Fax: (303) 839-1354
E-Mail: info@coloradokids.org

Connect for Kids. http://www.connectforkids.org
This site is an information/action center for anyone who wants to act on behalf of children. At this site you'll find a virtual encyclopedia of information on a variety of subjects concerning children. There is also an on-line press kit, a listing of current initiatives by state, a reference room, ideas for action, and a list of sponsoring and related organizations.

Council on Accreditation of Services for Families and Children, Inc. http://www.coanet.org
This international, non-profit organization is a standard setting accrediting body that has accredited more than 1200 providers in the United States and Canada. The COA has also established several national panels on standards and processes involving professionals, providers, funding sources, and consumers. This website contains information about the COA and how to contact them and information on their accreditation process. The contact information is:

COA
120 Wall Street, 11th Floor
New York, NY 10005
Tel: (212) 797-3000
Fax: (212) 797-1428
E-Mail: coanet@aol.com

The Division for Early Childhood. http://www.dec-sped.org
Part of the Council for Exceptional Children, the DEC advocates for individuals who work with children with special needs and their families. This website contains information about conferences, governmental information and action alerts, listservs, publications, positions statements and policies, information about exceptional children, the Journal of Early Intervention, and links to other related sites.

Focus Adolescent Services. http://www.focusas.com
This is a national adolescent treatment agency offers a wealth of information to help find services and resource to aid troubled teens and contains a number of

relevant articles, links to resources on the web, support for parents, a therapist directory, program and school information, and suggested reading. To contact call (877) 362-8727

HANDSNet. http://www.handsnet.org/
This is an online service, supported by organizations and individuals, designed to provide professionals and those interested in children's issues a wealth of information and resources. This website offers classes, strategic planning workshops, and management seminars as well as political information affecting human service providers and clients. There is also a working families roundtable, information on the National Campaign to End Gun Violence, and child poverty rates. There is also access to WebClipper which allows access to research on a variety of topics pertinent to human services.

Human Rights USA. http://www.hrusa.org
This organization works to educate people in the United States about their human rights and encourages community based action. This site contains information about the organization and current initiatives, information about advocacy, what's new, and an opportunity to search the site for specific information.

I Am Your Child Campaign. http://www.iamyourchild.org
This non-profit organizations' campaign for children is working to increase public awareness of early childhood issues, provide resources to families, and promote quality resources for children. This site contains information about the campaign, parenting tips, information about early childhood development and quality childcare (such as stages of development and the infant brain), and research and resources. To contact call: 1(888) 447-3400

Infact: Campaigning for Corporate Accountability. http://www.infact.org
This is a national grassroots corporate watchdog organization that is currently organizing the Tobacco Industry Campaign and the Hall of Shame Campaign. This site contains information about their campaigns and how to take action. There are also press releases, an annual report, a report on how the tobacco industry influences kids and a list of publications that can be ordered. To contact:
INFACT Campaign Headquarters

256 Hanover St.
Boston, MA 02113
Tel: (617) 742-4583
Fax: (617) 367-0191

Internet Nonprofit Center. http://nonprofits.org
This is an on-line resource for locating non-profit organizations throughout the country. To search you must know at least part of the name of the organization and the state it is located in. There is also a library of publications, information, and data about non-profit organizations, and links to funding sources.

Internet Online Summit: Focus on Children. http://www.kidsonline.org
In December 1997 over 300 organizations interested in the well-being of children gathered in Washington D.C. to address ways to assure that steps are taken to make the internet experience safe and educational for children. This website contains the information and reports produced from that summit as well as information about their current initiatives and a list of resources for parents.

Kids Growth. http://www.kidsgrowth.com
This site is a resource for parents by pediatricians and child care experts. There is a wealth of information about child development and child illnesses and well over a hundred online "doctor handouts" for parents on topics from allergies to vision. There are also resources for pediatricians, book reviews, and an opportunity to search the site for specific information. There is a section specifically for teens and teen health.

KidsPeace: The National Center for Kids Overcoming Crisis. http://www.kidspeace.org
This is a private, non-profit organization that provides public awareness of issues affecting children and treatment programs including the National Hospital for Kids in Crisis and KidsPeace National Centers for Kids in Crisis. KidsPeace is a member of the Child Welfare League of America. All information is in English, Spanish, German, and Japanese. Topics on the site include KidsPeace facts, crisis intervention, treatment programs, public education and the Healing Magazine. To contact KidsPeace: 1-(800) 8KID-123 or E-Mail at admissions@kidspeace.org.

National Black Child Development Institute. http://www.nbcdi.org
This non-profit organization works to improve and protect the quality of life of African American children and families. Their website contains information on current public policy issues, membership information, a resource center (which offers training programs on diversity, leadership, and mentoring) and information about their publications and annual conference. To contact the NBCDI write to:
National Black Child Development Institute
1023 15th Street, NW
Suite 600
Washington, D.C. 20005
Tel. (202) 387-1281
Fax: (202) 234-1738
E-Mail: moreinfor@nbcdi.org

National Center for Missing and Exploited Children. http://www.ncmec.org
This organization works to find and protect missing and exploited children. This site lists news and events, services, public education campaigns, success stories, and provides a "Child Alert" on-line database of missing children. There is also an education and resource section with child safety information and guides for families dealing with a missing child.

National Clearinghouse for Alcohol and Drug Information. http://www.health.org
This clearinghouse is a service of the Substance Abuse and Mental Health Services Administration of the U.S. Department of Health and Human Services. This site offers a substantial amount of information on the subjects of substance abuse and mental health. For example databases included are information about alcohol, smoking, drugs in the workplace, and access to MEDLINE. To contact:
The National Clearinghouse for Alcohol and Drug Information
P.O. Box 2345
Rockville, MD 20847-2345
Tel: (800) 729-6686
Fax: (301) 468-6433

National Coalition for the Homeless. http://nch.ari.net

This is a national advocacy network of homeless persons, activists, service providers, and others committed to ending homelessness through public education, policy advocacy, grassroots organizing, and technical assistance. This site contain a library of articles and books related to homelessness, including issues pertinent to children, directories of contact people, email addresses, and web pages of other organizations, Internet resources, legislation and policy, and information about NCH current projects. To contact:

National Coalition for the Homeless
1012 14th Street, NW #600
Washington, D.C. 20005-3410
Tel: (202) 737-6444
Fax: (202) 737-6445
E-Mail: nch@ari.net

National Directory of Children, Youth and Family Services. http://www.childrenyouthfamilydir.com

This is a comprehensive directory of over 22,000 state, county and independent agencies and services for children, families and youth. The directory identifies Human and Social Service agencies, Health and Medical Professionals and mental health providers, Juvenile and Family Court Judges, Juvenile Probation Officers, and Treatment Centers, Hospitals, Youth and Youth and Family Services Agencies. Sample pages of the directory and ordering instructions are available at the site.

National Early Childhood Technical Assistance System. http://www.nectas.unc.edu

This website is sponsored by the University of North Carolina at Chapel Hill and is a national technical assistance consortium that provides support to government agencies and others who are working to improve services to young children. This site contains information about the Individuals with Disabilities Education Act, Preschool Grants Program, a projects finder where you can search for intervention projects by topic or location, archives and publications, and an extensive list of links to related sites.

National Indian Child Welfare Association. http://www.nicwa.org/

This non-profit organization serves American Indian tribes to strengthen and enhance their child welfare services by providing culturally sensitive training and workshops, technical assistance, and assistance with needs assessments, program design and development, and tribal/state negotiations. NICWA also monitors public policy and legislation that impacts Native American children and maintains a large library of books and articles on child welfare and family issues. This website contains information about NICWA and their programs, public policy issues, current initiatives, membership information, catalog of publications such as the Indian Child Welfare Act Background Packet, and library search. To contact the NICWA:

National Indian Child Welfare Association
3611 SW Hood Street
Suite 210
Portland, OR 97201
Tel: (503) 222-4044
Fax: (503) 222-4007
E-Mail: info@nicwa.org

National Parent Information Network. http://npin.org

Sponsored by two ERIC Clearinghouses, the NPIN works to provide information to parents and those who work with parents and to foster the exchange of parenting materials. This site contains resources for parents with a special section for working parents and urban/minority parents, PARENTING-L an electronic discussion list, internet resources for and about parents, resources for those who work with parents, Parent News, a bi-monthly magazine, state networks for parents, and information about families, technology, and education.

National Parenting Association. http://www.parentsunite.org

This is a non-profit organization that works to help parents and children by providing advocacy and information about current issues affecting parents and children. This websites contains information about how to join the NPA, current issues affecting children and parents and their possible solutions, resources, and how parents can take action. The resources include books available on topics such as fatherhood and voting issues for parents. It also includes many links to topics such as working parents, child advocacy groups, and special interests for fathers. To contact the NPA write to:

National Parenting Association
51 W. 74th Street
Suite 1 B
New York, NY 10023
Tel. (212) 362-7575
Fax: (212) 362-1916

National Resource Center for Youth Services. http://www.nrcys.ou.edu/
This is located at the University of Oklahoma's College of Continuing Education and provides programs and services that support professionals who work in child welfare, youth services, and juvenile justice. This website contains information about upcoming training seminars and conferences, a catalog of publications as well as an on-line library, and information and referral services.

Prevention Yellow Pages. http://www.tyc.state.tx.us/prevention
This is a worldwide directory of programs, research, references, and resources dedicated to the prevention of youth problems and the promotion of nurturing children sponsored by the Texas Youth Commission. This site contains information in 54 subjects related to children such as abuse, education, drugs, violence, health, and many more. Reports can be downloaded with Adobe Acrobat Reader.

Pueblo Child Advocacy Center. http://www.puebloadvocacy.org
This organization is a coordinated effort of private and public child protection agencies in Pueblo, Colorado. This site contains information about child protection, reporting, investigation, court action, and child abuse. There is also a list of resources and links to related sites.

Route 6-16. http://www.cyberpatrol.com/616
Sponsored by The Learning Company, this is an on-line search engine for children, parents, and professionals focused on child well-being issues. This site offers more than 3,000 links and has been honored by the BBC as a "Top Site" on the Internet.

Search Institute. http://www.search-institute.org

This organization provides research benefiting children and youth. This site contains access to research in the areas of communities, families, schools, youth serving organizations, and policy. There is an opportunity to search the site for specific information and also a list of publications for many different professions from youth to policy makers, and resources and upcoming training sessions. To contact:

Search Institute
700 S. 3rd St.
Suite 210
Minneapolis, MN 55415-1138
Tel: (612) 376-8955
(800) 888-7828
E-Mail: si@search-institute.org

Social Work Search Engine. http://www.socialworksearch.com

This site is a search engine for information and resources found on the web that relate to social work including child welfare, adoption, foster care, mental health, violence, and other topics. Searches con be performed by broad topics or for specific information. There are also sections for what's new, what's recent, what's popular, and top searches.

Southern Institute on Children and Families. http://www.kidsouth.org/

This organization works to improve opportunities for children and families in the South, with particular attention paid to disadvantaged children. This site contains information on children's health, child care, transportation issues relevant to rural poor families, education, income support, and health insurance (such as statistics on uninsured children in southern states). There is also a section that offers a number of reports relating to these subjects and links to related sites. To contact:

The Southern Institute on Children and Families
620 Sims Ave.
Columbia, SC 29205
Tel: (803) 779-2607
Fax: (803) 254-6301

UNICEF. http://www.unicef.org

This world wide organization advocates and works for the protection of children's rights and to help the young meet their basic needs. This site contains statistics concerning children's issues in practically every country of the world, weekly updated news, information on children's rights, publications, archives, information about programs, and links to related sites. This website is in English, French, and Spanish.

YouthLink. http://www.youthlink.org

This is the communication center for the Youth in Action Campaign which is part of the Foundation of America, a non-profit organization that helps to improve the health, safety, and well being of children. The YouthLink website provides a forum to find out about issues affecting children and a way for youth to express their ideas about solutions to the problems youth are facing. The website contains a list of participating organizations, a list of supporters, and information on the National Youth Council. To contact them:

Foundation of America
43 Malaga Cove
Suite D
Palos Verdes, CA 90274

Zero to Three: National Center for Infants, Toddlers, and Families. http://www.zerotothree.org

This site offers a wealth of information for parents and professionals about infants, toddlers and families. The site includes information about child development, child care, child abuse and neglect, poverty and much more. There is also the results of current research, the National Training Institute, a newsroom, a resource list, and sponsorship opportunities. Additionally, there is a special section called "Brain Wonders" on the biological, social, emotional, and intellectual aspects of infant brain development. It is divided into sections for parents and professionals with tips for healthy brain development.

Chapter 16

STATISTICAL RESOURCES

Web sites listed in this section can all be found in other sections in this handbook, but have been compiled here because they all are major source of statistics about children. The descriptions of each should inform you as to the nature of the statistics a particular site offers. Fedstats, U.S. Census Bureau, and the American Humane Association websites are all excellent places to begin searching for statistics as they provide a wide variety of information about children, and the UNICEF web site is an excellent source for international statistics.

Administration for Children and Families. http://www.acf.dhhs.gov/programs/acyf/
This is part of the U.S. Department of Health and Human Services and administers the major Federal programs the serve at risk children and their families. Within the ACF is the Administration on Children, Youth and Families, which is divided into four bureaus: ChildCare Bureau, Children's Bureau, Family and Youth Services Bureau, and Head Start Bureau. The ACYF also provides research demonstration and evaluation. The website offers a wealth of information about ACYF programs and research outcomes.

Agency for Health Care Policy and Research. http://www.ahcpr.gov
This is the lead agency charged with supporting research designed to improve the quality of health care, reduce it's cost, and broaden access to essential services. This website contains funding opportunities, research findings on a variety of

health care related topics including clinical information, and statistics. The Child and Adolescent Health page includes information on current research, the child health advisory group, tools and resources for measuring quality, and specific topics such as children with chronic conditions.

American Humane Association. http://www.americanhumane.org
This is a non-profit organization that works to help both animals and children. The Children's Division helps to improve public and private child welfare agencies by providing national Roundtables and Institutes on current issues affecting children, advocacy, and research and program analysis. This website contains a wealth of information about current initiatives, publications, research services, training and education, membership information, legislation, and links to other sites. To contact the AHA write to:
American Humane Association
63 Inverness Drive East
Englewood, CO 80112-5117
Tel: (303) 792-9900

Bureau of Justice Statistics. http://www.ojp.usdoj.gov/bjs/
This is a component of the U.S. Department of Justice and provides statistics and information about criminal offenders (and juveniles), crimes and victims, and the justice system. The BJS also provides data for analysis and on-line access to Crime and Justice Data Abstracts and online tabulations, datasets, and codebooks. To contact the BJS:
Bureau of Justice Statistics
810 Seventh Street, NW
Washington, DC 20531
Tel: (202) 307-0765
E-Mail: askbjs@ojp.usdoj.gov

Bureau of Labor Statistics. http://www.bls.gov
This website is part of the U.S. Department of labor and contains data, the economy at a glance, regional information, publications and research papers which includes reports on the youth labor force and welfare to work programs, surveys and programs, links to other statistical sites, and K-12 educational resources.

Bureau of Transportation Statistics. http://www.bts.gov
This site is part of the U.S. Department of Transportation and contains airline information, commodity flow survey, databases, geographic information services, statistical policy and research, and a the bureau of transportation kids web page.

Campaign for Our Children. www.cfoc.org
This organization is a joint effort of public and private agencies who work to provide advocacy and education on issues affecting children and teenagers. This site contains useful information on programs and advocacy campaigns aimed at improving the welfare of America's children. There is a parent resource section, technical support, teacher resources, a press room, a catalog of publications, facts and statistics, and a special section addressing teen pregnancy.

Center for Disease Control and Prevention. http://www.cdc.gov
This website provides health data and statistics, information about grants other funding opportunities, links to other sites, and an opportunity to subscribe to their health publications. There is also an extensive online database of health related topics which offers n opportunity to search for information on health topics related to adolescent and teen or infants and children.

Center for Mental Health Services. http://www.mentalhealth.org/cmhs
This agency is part of the Substance Abuse and Mental Health Services Administration and leads Federal efforts to treat mental illnesses and increase the quality and range of treatment, rehabilitation, and support services for people with mental illnesses, their families, and communities. This site contains information on the children's campaign including the 1997 annual report, emergency services, community supports, mental health statistics and funding. It also has an extensive list of online publications on such topics as teen mental health, caring for your child, and a family guide for children with mental health needs.

Child Abuse Prevention Network. http://child.cornell.edu/capn.html
Sponsored by LifeNet, Inc. and Cornell University's Family Life Development Center, this site is the world wide nerve center for professional in the field of child abuse and neglect. This site contains direct links to the major resources of child abuse information, statistics, link to the National Data Archive

on Child Abuse and Neglect, child abuse research such as prevention resources, listservs to stay current on hot issues, and links to federal child abuse resources.

ChildHelp USA. http://www.childhelpusa.org

This organization is dedicated to meeting the physical, emotional, and spiritual needs of abused and neglected children focusing efforts and resources upon treatment, prevention, and research. This site contains information about child abuse, a national child abuse hotline, information on reporting child abuse, a list of nationwide facilities, statistics on child abuse in America including victims and perpetrators, resources, and referrals. To contact:

ChildHelp USA National Headquarters
15757 N. 78th St.
Scottsdale, AZ 85260
Tel: (602) 922-8212

Children's Defense Fund. http://www.childrensdefense.org

This is a non-profit, private organization that works to serve the needs of children through advocacy, research, and support for child welfare agencies. This website contains information about children's issues, the Black Community Crusade for Children, news and reports on children, a list of publications including A Parents Guide to Child Support, and the CDF Book Nook. There are pages and detailed information on health and mental health, economic, education, safety, and religious issues that relate to children and the Childrens Defense Fund's involvement in each of these areas. To contact the CDF national headquarters:

Children's Defense Fund
25 E Street NW
Washington, DC 20001
Tel: (202) 628-8787
E-Mail: cdinfo@childrensdefense.org

Children's Health Indicators. http://www.ed.gov/pubs/YouthIndicators/ Health.html

From the U.S. Department of Education, this site contains a number of tables and graphs charting the number of children involved in a variety of health related issues, such as insurance, AIDS knowledge, physical fitness, violence, tobacco, alcohol, and drug use.

Coalition for Asian-American Children and Families. http://www.cacf.org
This is a private, non-profit organization that advocates for Asian-American children and families and works to help health and human service providers address the changing needs of the Asian-American community. This website provides information about issues affecting Asian-American children and families and a comprehensive directory for Asian-American children and families. There is also a list of myths and facts about Asian-Americans, issues of their quarterly newsletter, membership information, statistics related to health and education, a list of funding sources, a new Asian Kids InfoLink, and links to other websites.

Department of Health and Human Services Data Council. http://aspe.os. dhhs.gov/datacncl
This organization coordinates all health and non-health data collection and analysis activities of the Department of Health and Human Services, including an integrated health data collection strategy, coordination of health data standards, and health information and privacy policy activities.

Family Preservation and Child Welfare Network. http://www.family preservation.com
From the South Carolina Department of Social Services, this site contains the mission and goals of the organization, information on child abuse and neglect, foster care, adoption, family violence, and federal child and family statistics. There is also a photolist of waiting children and information on fetal abuse and childhood disabilities.

Fedstats. http://www.fedstats.gov
This site contains statistics from more than 70 U.S. Federal Government agencies, such as the Enviormental Protection Agency or the National Center for Education Statistics (see below). This site can be searched by agency, program, region, or topic. There are also press releases, fast facts, and additional links to related sites.

Health Care Financing Administration. http://www.hcfa.gov
This is the federal agency that administers the Medicare, Medicaid, and Child Health Insurance Programs. This site contains information and reports on these health care programs, information on projects and initiatives of the HCFA,

statistics and data, research information, an information clearinghouse, laws and regulations, and links to other government sites.

Injury Control Resource Information Network. www.injurycontrol. com/icrin/

This site is sponsored by the Center for Injury Prevention and Control at the University of Pittsburgh and is a way to access on-line resources related to the field of injury research and control. The site contains a slide show of ICRIN's structure, content, and benefits and information from the site can be translated form English to Spanish. Information available includes injury data and statistics, publications, injury specific resources such as preventing injuries at school, recent research, grant opportunities, software and related research tools, and links to government and related sites.

March of Dimes. http://www.modimes.org

This organization works to improve the health of babies by preventing birth defects and infant mortality. This website can be viewed in both English and Spanish and provides infant health statistics, birth defects information, a resource center, program information, research and a health library.

National Adoption Information Clearinghouse. http://www.calib.com/naic/

This is a service of the Children's Bureau, Administration on Children, Youth and Families, Administration for Children and Families, and the Department of Health and Human Services and provides a wealth of information about adoption. This site contains online databases (such as their bibliographic database, national organization directory), online publications, information about funding, adoption statistics, introductory packages for prospective adoptive parents, a conference calendar, and links to related sites. There is also a list of NAIC publications including a guide to adoption sites on the internet and an adoption library containing research reports and studies on all aspects of adoption. To contact the NAIC:

National Adoption Information Clearinghouse
330 C Street, SW
Washington, D.C. 20447
Tel: (888) 251-0075
(703) 352-3488

Fax: (703) 385-3206
E-Mail: naic@calib.com

National Center for Children in Poverty. http://cpmcnet.columbia.edu/ dept/nccp
This organization is sponsored by Columbia University and works to promote strategies that reduce child poverty and improve life chance of those children who are living in poverty. This site contains information related to child poverty, including statistics for state and local poverty, reports on childcare and early education, family support and welfare reform, publications, and resources. There is a comprehensive program summary that discusses the nature of poverty's impact on children. To contact:
National Center for Children in Poverty
The Joseph L. Mailman School of Public Health
Columbia University
154 Haven Ave.
New York, NY 10032
Tel: (212) 304-7100
Fax: (212) 544-4200
(212) 544-4201

National Center for Education Statistics. http://nces.ed.gov
This website is part of the U.S. Department of Education and provides a large amount of statistics relating to education. The site includes a electronic catalog of the most recently released publications and data products, fast facts, and a special section for kids to search for schools and colleges.

It also includes an encyclopedia of education statistics, and extensive survey and program areas section which includes surveys of elementary, secondary and postsecondary institutions as well as longitudinal surveys and education assessments.

National Center for Health Statistics. http://www.cdc.gov/nchs
This site is sponsored by the Center for Disease Control and Prevention and contains a large amount of statistics on a variety of health related subjects. These include a report on key indicators of well being in America's children, children growth charts, and access to many data sets such as the National Health Interview Survey. The site also offers links to other statistics websites, a data warehouse, surveys and data collection systems, publications and news releases.

National Committee on Vital and Health Statistics. http://www.ncvhs.hhs.gov
This committee provides advice and assistance to the Department of Health and Human Services and serves as a forum for interaction with interested private sector groups on a variety of key health data issues. Included in this site is a calendar, a list of subcommittees, reports and recommendations for the past several years, transcripts of recent meetings, hot topics, and of course statistics on a variety of subjects.

National Institute of Child Health and Human Development. http://www.nichd.nih.gov/
This organization is part of the National Institute of Health and conducts and supports laboratory, clinical, and epidemiological research on the reproductive, neurobiology, developmental, and behavioral processes that determine and maintains the health of children, families, adults, and populations. This site contains information about what's new with the NICHD, funding by NICHD, intramural research, epidemiology statistics and prevention, publications clearinghouse, and employment and fellowship opportunities. It also includes research resources such as access to survey data sets from the Demographic and Behavioral Sciences Branch as well as the Cochchrane Neonatal Collaborative Review Group which posts results from neonatal studies.

National Institute of Health. http://www.nih.gov
This site contains an overview of this government agency as well as a calendar of events, health publications, clinical trials, a guide to diseases under investigation at NIH, information about grants including application kits and research contracts, on-line journals, and on-line research labs. Institutes within NIH include the National Institute of Drug Abuse, the National Institute of Mental

Health, the National Institute of Alcohol Abuse and Alcoholism, and the National Institute of Child Health and Human Development (see above). To contact:
Harold Varmus, Director
National Institute of Health
Bethesda, MD 20892

National Longitudinal Study of Adolescent Health. http://www.cpc.unc.edu/addhealth/
This is a study being performed by the Carolina Population Center at the University of North Carolina at Chapel Hill of the health related behaviors of Adolescents in grades 7-12. This site contains information about the study, data sets, codebooks, publications and presentations, and much more. The study includes nationwide data from over 90,000 school age children (although the public can only access up to 50% of this data). The site also includes access to a data analysis assistance service.

Occupational Safety and Health Administration. http://www.osha.gov
This agency is part of the U.S. Department of Labor and works to save lives, prevent injuries, and protect the health of American workers. This site includes a news room, OSHA regulations, technical links and training information, and a library that contains statistics and data, manuals, and reports.

Substance Abuse and Mental Health Services Administration. http://www.samhsa.gov
This agency is part of the U.S. Department of Health and Human Services and works to provide substance abuse and mental health services. This site contains substance abuse and mental health information and statistics (such as household survey on drug abuse, substance abuse facility treatment finder, and an analytic series, which includes topics such as teenage drinking and mental health). It also includes information on grants, program information, and links to six special offices that focus on specific areas such as the Office of Managed Care and the Office on Aids and a clearinghouse. There are also news releases, an opportunity to search the site for specific information and media services.

UNICEF. http://www.unicef.org

The United Nations Children's Fund advocates and works for the protection of children's rights and to help the young meet their basic needs. This site contains statistics concerning children's issues (such as mortality, immunization, nutrition and education) in practically every country of the world, weekly updated news, information on children's rights, publications, archives, information about programs, and links to related sites. This website is in English, French, and Spanish.

U.S. Census Bureau. http://www.census.gov

This site provides social, demographic, and economic information about the population. Searches can be done by state or by subjects listed from "A to Z". There is also a product catalog, links to related and minority sites, and a number of reports that can be downloaded.

U.S. Department of Education. http://www.ed.gov

This site contains a wealth of information related to education including funding opportunities, financial aid information, research and statistics, programs and services, a list of publications and products, the department of education's budget, and links to other sites. Some of the publications available through this site include the department wide initiatives for 2000, the special education and individuals with disabilities act, and elementary and secondary education and early childhood reports. You can also access National Center for Education Statistics (see above) which includes an encyclopedia of statistics, survey and program areas and information on assessment. To contact:

U.S. Department of Education
400 Maryland Ave., SW Washington, D.C. 20202-4098
Tel: (800) USA-LEARN
E-Mail: CustomerService@met.ed.gov

U.S. Department of Health and Human Services. http://www.os.dhhs.gov/

This is the governments principal agency for protecting the health of all Americans and provides services for the many populations, including children. Some selected topics related to children on this site are: adoption, child care, child support enforcement, children's health insurance, and teen pregnancy. This website provides extensive information about current issues and programs for a number of populations as well as current research, policy information, employee

information, and links to other HHS agencies. The HHS headquarters is located at:
Hubert H. Humphrey Building
200 Independence Ave., SW
Washington, DC 20201

The Urban Institute. http://www.urban.org
This organization investigates social and economic problems confronting the nation and analyzes efforts to solve these problems. This site contains useful resources on policy issues and an analysis of the State Children's Health Insurance Program. There is access to research by topic and author and a number of reports on a variety of subjects which include at risk teens, children at risk, and child care in America. There is also access to recent news articles published by the institute. To contact:
The Urban Institute
2100 M Street, NW
Washington, D.C. 20037
Tel: (202) 833-7200

Youth Indicators 1993. http://www.ed.gov/pubs/YouthIndicators/index.html
This site contains information on the trends in well-being of American youth from the National Center for Education Statistics and the U.S. Department of Education. Categories are home, school, health, citizenship and values, and future. Statistics reported include: demographics and family composition, family income, school description, school outcomes, out of school experiences, health, citizenship and values.

Chapter 17

FOUNDATIONS SPECIALIZING IN CHILDREN'S ISSUES

There are countless number of foundation and philanthropies that provide funding for organizations working to improve child well-being, far too many to be included in this handbook. This section however, contains a few of the prominent foundations helping children's organizations, as well as a few on-line resources that provide a far more comprehensive list of foundations. The Foundation Center web site is perhaps the best resource on the internet for finding funding sources and help with grant writing. Also, several foundations offer links and lists of other foundations and may be worth exploring.

Aspen Publishers, Inc. http://www.aspenpublishers.com
   This publishing company recently released GrantScape, a database on nearly 15,000 private, community, and corporate foundations, and features a search engine to target qualified donors quickly. This can be ordered from the publishing company for a fee. To contact:
   Aspen Publishers
   7201 McKinney Circle
   P.O. Box 990
   Frederick, MD 21705-9727
   Tel: (800) 638-8437

The Annie E. Casey Foundation. http://www.aecf.org/kidscount

This is a private foundation that works to track the status of children on a state and national level and provides grants to those who are interested in serving the needs of children. This website contains a wealth of information about the foundation as well as a number of reports on the status of children and the results of their annual Kids Count report. Also on the website are the grant guidelines, information about child care workers salaries, child care model programs and policies, contacts for state Kids Count projects, and information about their current initiatives. To contact them:

The Annie E. Casey Foundation
701 St. Paul St.
Baltimore, MD 21202
Tel: (410) 547-6600
Fax: (410) 547-6624
E-Mail: webmail@aecf.org

Benton Foundation. http://www.benton.org

This is a philanthropy that is interested in helping people through public policy, community action, and communications. This site contains information about communications policy and practice, an on-line network for artists and arts organizations, a publications catalog, a special section for kids, and networking for better health care. It also includes Connect for Kids a resource for adults to get information on how to assist children, this includes social and political information as well as on-line discussion sessions. To contact:

Benton Foundation
1634 Eye St. NW
Washington, D.C. 20006
Tel: (202) 638-5770
Fax: (202) 638-5771
E-Mail: benton@benton.org

California Community Foundation. http://www.calfund.org

This organization is a source of grant support for non-profit organizations in the greater Los Angeles area to help the disadvantaged and those discriminated against. This site contains their annual report, a list of publications (such as annual reports, and surveys), information about grants and grantmaking, press releases, and links to related sites.

Carnegie Foundation. http://www.carnegie.org

This site contains information about the foundation, what's new, an overview of their programs, information about special initiatives including the task force on meeting the needs of young children, Carnegie Council on Adolescent development, and Starting Points State and Community Partnerships for Young Children. There are also grant restrictions and proposals, corporation news, other foundation and non-profit resources, and access to the corporation's archives. To contact:

Carnegie Corporation of New York
437 Madison Ave.
New York, NY 10022
Tel: (212) 371-3200
Fax: (212) 754-4073

Charles Stewart Mott Foundation. http://www.mott.org

This is a philanthropy that provides grants to organizations who address four main topics: civil society, environment, poverty, and improving Flint, MI. This site contains information about the foundation, a list of publications, information about the grant making process, and information about programs addressing their four main areas of interest. You can also access Mott's grant database from 1995-1999 and search by topic or geographic area. To contact:

Charles Stewart Mott Foundation
1200 Mott Foundation Building
Flint, MI 48502-1851
Tel: (810) 238-5651
Fax: (810) 766-1753
Publications Request Line: (800) 645-1766
Or (414) 273-9643
E-Mail: infocenter@mott.org

The Commonwealth Fund. http://www.cmwf.org
The fund's current four national program areas are improving health care, bettering the health of minority Americans, advancing the well-being of elderly people, and developing the capacities of children and young people. The child health program web page offers detailed information about current programs and recent grants in the area of child health. This website contains a publication list, information about current programs, surveys, annual report, a number of reports on the state of Medicaid and other health concerns, and grant guidelines.

The Danny Foundation. http://www.dannyfoundation.org
This philanthropy's mission is to prevent unintentional injuries, conduct research, and provide leadership to set regulatory standards for safe nursery products. This site contains information about the history of the foundation, information about crib laws and dangers, the newsletter, alerts and recalls, fundraising and development efforts, safety tips, and links to other sites.
To contact:
The Danny Foundation
P.O. Box 680
Alamo, CA 94507
Tel: (800) 83-DANNY
E-Mail: dannycrib@earthlink.com

The David and Lucille Packard Foundation. http://www.packfound.org
This foundation supports non-profit organizations through the improvement of scientific knowledge, education, health, culture, employment opportunities, the environment, and quality of life. This site contains the 1999 guidelines, an annual report, Y2K information for non-profits, and a number of on-line journals that can be downloaded such as the Future of Children Journal. To contact:
The David and Lucille Packard Foundation
300 Second St., Suite 200
Los Altos, CA 94022
Tel: (650) 948-7658

Ford Foundation. http://www.fordfound.org
This philanthropy is a resource for individuals and institutions who strengthen democratic values, reduce poverty and injustice, promote international

cooperation, and advance human achievement. The areas of focus are: asset building and community development, peace and social justice, education, media, arts, and culture. This site contains a grants database, guidelines for grant seekers, information about the foundation and it's programs, a list of publications (annual reports, quarterly magazine, and recent publications) and news. To contact:
Ford Foundation
320 East 43rd St.
New York, NY 10017
Tel: (212) 573-5000
Fax: (212) 351-3677

The Foundation Center. http://www.fdncenter.org
This is a nonprofit information clearinghouse that helps organizations and individuals learn about foundations and the grant making process. This site contains a library of materials on philanthropy, on line courses in grant writing, access to 990-PF tax forms, grantmaker materials, periodicals and books, and bibliographic literature. They will also give research advice and, for a fee, perform custom searches. To contact:
The Foundation Center
79 Fifth Ave.
New York, NY 10003-3076
Tel: (212) 620-4230

The Frank Stanley Beveridge Foundation, Inc. http://www.beveridge.org
This philanthropy is for religious, charitable, scientific, literary or educational purposes or for the prevention of cruelty to children. The site contains information about the philanthropy, the grant funding cycle, how to request a grant and the limitations and eligibility guidelines, as well as other funding sources.

Hearst Foundation. http://fdncenter.org/grantmaker/hearst
The information about this foundation is available through the Foundation Center's website. This philanthropy provides grants for education, health, social services and culture. This site also includes funding priorities, funding policies, and information about applying for a grant. To contact:
The William Randolph Hearst Foundation
East of the Mississippi   West of the Mississippi

888 7th Ave. 45th Floor
New York, NY 10106-0057
Tel: (212) 586-5404

90 New Montgomery St., Suite 1212
San Francisco, CA 94105-4504
Tel: (415) 543-0400

Kaiser Family Foundation. http://www.kff.org

This is an independent health care philanthropy that focuses on four main areas: health policy, reproductive health, HIV policy, and health and development in South Africa. This site contains information about these four subjects as well as state health facts, a link library, surveys, the Kaiser Commission of Medicaid and the Uninsured, and an on-line grant application. To contact:

Kaiser Family Foundation
2400 Sand Hill Rd.
Menlo Park, CA 94025
Tel: (650) 854-9400
Fax: (650) 854-4800

The McKnight Foundation. http://www.mcknight.org

This is a private philanthropy that provides funding to non-profit organizations and public agencies in the following areas: children, families, and communities, arts, environment, initiatives, research and applied science, and international programs. This site contains information about current programs, news, how to apply, and publications such as annual reports and task force reports etc.

Robert Wood Johnson Foundation. http://www.rwjf.org

This is the nation's largest philanthropy devoted to health care. This site includes information about the foundation, current projects and programs, information about applying for grants, media information such as press releases, grant results and outcomes, and resource centers such as Chronic Net which as an on-line resource for chronic health conditions. To contact:

The Robert Wood Johnson Foundation
P.O. Box 2316
College Road East and Rt. 1
Princeton, NJ 08543-2316
Tel: (609) 452-8701
E-Mail: mail@rwjf.org

Schwab Foundation. http://www.schwablearning.org

This philanthropy is dedicated to raising awareness about learning differences and providing parents and teachers with the information, resources, and support they need to improve the lives of children. This website offers customized information and individual responsiveness from professional resource consultants, librarians, and information specialists on-line and over the phone for anyone who has concerns and questions about learning differences. There are also resources for parents, teachers, and the media. To contact:

Schwab Foundation for Learning
1650 South Amphlett Blvd., Suite 3000
San Mateo, CA 94402
Tel: (800) 230-0988
(650) 655-2410
Fax: (650) 655-2411

W.K. Kellogg Foundation. http://www.wkkf.org

This organization works to help individual, communities, and organizations build the capacity to solve problems. Specifically, the foundation is interested in funding projects within the United States, Caribbean, and South Africa. This site contains information about current projects such as Community Voices: Healthcare for the Underserved. There is also available a number of publications and papers, an on-line annual report, resources, journals, programming interests, an evaluation handbook, and information on how to apply for a grant. To contact:

W.K. Kellogg Foundation
One Michigan Ave. East
Battle Creek, MI 49017-4058
Tel: (616) 968-1611

W.T Grant Foundation. http://fdncenter.org/grantmaker/wtgrant /98ar08.html

Information about this philanthropy can be found at the Foundation Center's website. The purpose of this foundation is to assist research, education, and training in order to improve the well-being of children, adolescents, and youth. Included in this site is information about the application procedure, cover sheet for letters of inquiry, a list of 1996 grants awarded, an annual report, and information about their programs.

Chapter 18

Professional Organizations for Children

Most professionals in child related fields belong to at least one professional organization. Many of these associations have conferences, journals, newsletters, and are excellent resources for locating information about current trends and experts in their field. The following list is a summary of the web sites for many of the major national child centered organizations.

Alliance for Children and Families. http://alliance1.org
This international non-profit organization is made up of over 350 child and family serving organizations. This website contains information resources on families, grant development, marketing, public policy interpretation, volunteer leadership and more. There is also information about peer networking and education, research, programming, and operations and management assistance. It is a membership site but you can still access much of the information without being a member.

American Academy of Adoption Attorneys. http://adoptionattorneys.org
This is a national association of attorneys who practice in the field of adoption law. This website offers a way to search for an Academy Attorney, membership information, media information (this includes position statements, an adoption glossary, and adoption facts), and public information. To contact:
American Academy of Adoption Attorneys

P.O. Box 33053
Washington, DC 20033-0053
Tel: (202) 832-2222

American Academy of Child and Adolescent Psychiatry. http://www.aacap.org

This organization provides information useful to understanding developmental, behavioral, emotional, and mental disorders affecting children and adolescents. This website offers information about membership, information and resources for families, press releases, information about current legislation, journal and other publications, a list of regional organizations, information about training seminars, job listings, and links to other websites. To contact the AACAP write to:

The American Academy of Child and Adolescent Psychiatry
3615 Wisconsin Avenue, NW
Washington, D.C. 20016-2891
Tel: (202) 966-7300
Fax: (202) 966-2891

American Academy of Pediatrics. http://www.aap.org

This is a nonprofit organization of professional members that provides, advocacy, education, research, and services that improve pediatric care. This website has a wealth of information about public policy and child health care. There are monthly policy statements as well as practical information about children's health and safety, such as a shopping guide for car seats. Also available through the website is information about professional education, current research, publications, current press releases, membership information and an extensive list of agency contacts, as well as a book store. To contact the AAP National Headquarters:

The American Academy of Pediatrics
141 Northwest Point Boulevard
Elk Grove Village, IL 60007-1098
Tel: (847) 228-5005
Fax: (847) 228-5097

American Association for Marriage and Family Therapy. http://www.aamft.org

This is a professional association for the field of marriage and family therapy. This website contains information about the association, membership information, information about marriage and family therapy, a way to search for a therapist, clinical updates, resources for practitioners, and information about families and health. They also have a Consumer Update on various mental health and developmental issues such as Attention Deficit Hyperactivity Disorder. You can access the archives to see older Consumer Update newsletters as well. To contact:

American Association for Marriage and Family Therapy
1133 15th Street, NW
Suite 300
Washington, DC 20005-2710
Tel: (202) 452-0109

American Association of Family and Consumer Services. http://www.aafcs.org

This is the only national organization representing family and consumer sciences professionals across practice areas and across content specialties. Specifically, this organization seeks to improve individual and family wellbeing by influencing delivery of services and policy in areas related to family. This site contains information about the organization and membership, professional development, awards, fellowships and grants, publications and products, and news and activities. To contact:

American Association of Family and Consumer Services
1555 King Street
Alexandria, VA 22314
Tel: (703) 706-4600
Fax: (703) 706-4663
E-Mail: info@aafcs.org

American Association of School Administrators. http://www.aasa.org

This is a national professional organization of school administrators and other school leaders. This website contains membership information, an education marketplace, on-line editions of the AASA's publications such as Back Fence for rural schools or Edge City for suburban schools, a list of state associations, awards

and scholarships, a job bulletin, current events and ideas, and advocacy information. To contact:
   American Association of School Administrators
   1801 North Moore Street
   Arlington, VA 22209
   Tel: (703) 528-0700
   Fax: (703) 841-1543

American Association on Mental Retardation. http://www.aamr.org
   This is the oldest interdisciplinary organization of professionals concerned with mental retardation and other disabilities. This site contains membership information, a list of events, professional resources, a directory of state and regional chapters, a bookstore, abstracts, an extensive list of special interest groups including one dedicated to families and mental retardation, and a wealth of other information related to mental retardation. To contact:
   AAMR
   444 North Capital Street, NW
   Suite 846
   Washington, DC 20001-1512
   Tel: (202) 387-1968
   (800) 424-3688
   Fax: (202) 387-2193

American Bar Association Center on Children and the Law. http://www.abanet.org/child
   This center works to improve laws and policies affecting children, research and provide information on laws, policies, and practices affecting children, and increase public awareness of law and justice issues that relate to children. These issues are specific in the areas of child abuse and neglect, child welfare, foster care, child abductions, child and adolescent health issues, substance abuse and child protection, and legal representation of children, parents, and child welfare agencies. This website contains a wealth of information about children and the law and has a number of reports and current legislation that can be downloaded such as child welfare laws, state child abuse laws, child welfare tips, and child protection law reform. Also on the website is a list of publications and periodicals, the annual report, internship opportunities, discussion groups, a factbook, lawyer

standards, and links to other ABA sites as well as to other agency sites. To contact the ABA:
American Bar Association
750 Lake Shore Dr.
Chicago, IL 60611
Tel: (302) 988-5000
E-Mail: info@abanet.org

American College of Nurse-Midwives. http://midwife.org
This organization promotes the health and well being of women and provides research, accredits nurse-midwifery education programs, administers and promotes continuing education, and establishes clinical practice standards. This site offers professional information, midwifery education and career counseling, a search engine to find a nurse-midwife, a press room, documents, web resources, political action, and products, events, and services. To contact:
American College of Nurse-Midwives
818 Connecticut Avenue, NW
Suite 900 Washington, DC 20006
Tel: (202) 728-9860
Fax: (202) 728-9897
E-Mail: info@acnm.org

American Counseling Association. http://www.counseling.org
This professional organization works to promote the field of counseling through advocacy, research and creating professional standards. This site contains membership information, employment opportunities, papers and other publications, a special section for students in counseling education, on-line continuing education, a calendar of events, and news and information about the field which include child related issues. To contact:
American Counseling Association
5999 Stevenson Ave.
Alexandria, VA 22304
Tel: (703) 823-9800
Fax: (703) 823-0252

American Medical Association. http://www.ama-assn.org
This is a membership organization of physicians that works to advocate for patients and physicians. This site includes a Family Focus section and KidsHealth page that provide information on topics such as children's nutrition, safety and accident prevention, baby development, childhood infections, and emergencies and first aid. There is also the National Patient Safety Foundation, an on-line library, and on-line publication (for members).

American Nurses Association. http://www.nursingworld.org
This is a professional organization of 2.6 million nurses and 13 organizational affiliate members. This site contains a wealth of information about nursing and nursing related issues. There is also a bookstore, membership information, nursing links, a reference and reading room, nursing standards, ethics, on-line journals, and links to affiliate nursing organizations such as the American Nurses Foundation and the American Academy of Nursing. To contact:
American Nurses Association
600 Maryland Ave., SW
Suite 100 West
Washington, DC 20024
Tel: (800) 274-4ANA

American Professional Society on the Abuse of Children. http://www.apsac.org
This is an interdisciplinary organization made up of professionals who are concerned with child maltreatment and provides a forum for discussing professional issues, encourages research, and provides information on current child maltreatment issues to professionals. This website provides information about the organization and state chapters, professional education, legislation (such as the Safe Adoption and Family Envrionments Act and the Child Abuse Prevention and Treatment Act), publications, memberships, public affairs, and how to make a donation.

American Psychoanalytic Association. http://www.APSA.org
This is a professional association of psychoanalysts and is comprised of the Affiliate Societies and Training Institutes throughout the country. This site contains a virtual bookshop, an opportunity to do a literature search, information

about psychoanalysis and their fellowship program, committee and task force information, a way to search for an analyst, and *The American Psychoanalyst* and *JAPA* online. It also includes general information about psychoanalysis as well as psychoanalysis for children and adolescents. To contact:

American Psychoanalytic Association
309 East 49th Street
New York, NY 10017
Tel: (212) 752-0450
Fax: (212) 593-0571
E-Mail: central.office@apsa.org

American Psychological Association. http://www.apa.org

This is the website of the APA and contains a wealth of information for psychologists and other professions working in related fields. There are also sections for parents and teens addressing a number of subjects such as parenting, healthcare and depression, a section about children, as well as a student section. There is an opportunity to search the site for specific information and access to psychological databases. There is a research office that collects and disseminates research information and an on-line newsletter. In addition there is access to videos on a wide range of topics and links to international affiliate organizations.

American Public Health Association. http://www.apha.org

This site contains a substantial amount of information about legislation and advocacy, public health resources, practice and policy as they relate to public health. APHA includes special interest groups such as maternal and child health which have there own homepages that can be accessed from this site. There is also information about continuing education, membership, and affiliates and caucuses. To contact the APHA:

American Public Health Association
800 1st street, NW
Washington, D.C. 20001-3710
Tel: (202) 777-2742
Fax: (202) 777-2534
E-Mail: comments@alsph.org

American Public Human Services Association. http://www.aphsa.org

This is a non-profit organization that works to improve public human service policies by providing education and information about child welfare, health care reform, and the elderly. This website contains information about APHSA publications, state and local news and issues, welfare reform, conferences, and how to join as well as links to other sites, a job bank, and a WebBoard, which includes a chat room.

American School Counselor Association. http://www.schoolcounselor.org

This membership organization is made up of more than 12,000 school counseling professionals and is focused on providing professional development, enhancing school counseling programs, and researching effective school counseling practices. This site contains the national standards for school counseling programs, a role statement for the school counselor, violence prevention resources, a government relations program, membership information, and benefits and services information. To contact:

ASCA801 North Fairfax Street, Suite 310
Alexandria, VA 22314
Tel: (800) 306-4722
Fax: (703) 683-1619
E-Mail: asca@erols.com

Association of Teacher Educators. http://www.siu.edu/departments/coe/ate/

This is a national membership organization devoted to improving teacher education for school and campus-based teachers. This web site contains information about the organization, a list of upcoming events, membership information, media resources, ATE standards for teacher educators, ATE special interest groups (these provide more detailed information on such topics as middle school education, learning styles, multicultural education, special education, science education etc.), ATE positions and resolutions, ATE strategic planning document, and links to related sites. To contact:

Association of Teacher Educators
Executive Director
1900 Association Drive, Suite ATE
Reston, VA 20191-1502
Tel: (703) 620-3110

Fax: (703) 620-9530
E-Mail: ATE1@AOL.com

Council for Exceptional Children. http://www.cec.sped.org
This is the largest international professional organization dedicated to improving educational outcomes for gifted, exceptional, or disabled individuals. This website contains information on professional standards, recognition and accreditation, career connections, public policy and legislative information, and a CEC discussion forum. CEC also manages the Educational Resources Information Clearinghouse for Exceptional Children, and other institutes for research and training in areas such as bilingual education, and education of children with disabilities. To contact:
The Council for Exceptional Children (CEC)
1920 Association Drive
Reston, VA 20191-1589
Voice phone: 703-620-3660 local or 1-888-CEC-SPED toll free
TTY: 703-264-9446
FAX: 703-264-9494

International Society for the Prevention of Child Abuse and Neglect. http://ispcan.org
This is an interdisciplinary international organization of professional who work towards the prevention and treatment of child abuse, neglect, and exploitation globally. This site contains an overview of the organization, training events, membership information (which includes a quarterly newsletter and monthly journal, and links to related sites). This organization is funded by membership and sponsors and contributors. To contact:
International Society for the Prevention of Child Abuse and Neglect
200 N. Michigan Ave., Suite 500
Chicago, IL 60601
Tel: (312) 578-1401
Fax: (312) 578-1405
E-Mail: ISPCAN@AOL.com

National Alliance for the Mentally Ill. http://www.nami.org

This is a grassroots organization of primarily families and consumers of the mental health system as well as some mental health professionals that focuses on the unmet needs of people suffering from debilitating mental illnesses. This website contains policy information, a press room, information about youth, links to affiliate organizations, a book store, a helpline, and much more. The information about youth includes NAMI's position statement on early onset brain disorders, early intervention programs, violence prevention, as well as general information childhood and adolescent mental health. To contact:

National Alliance for the Mentally Ill
200 North Glebe Rd., Suite 1015
Arlington, VA 22203-3754
Tel: (703) 524-7600
(800) 950-NAMI
Fax: (703) 524-9094

National Association for the Education of Young Children. http://www.naeyc.org

This is an organization of early childhood professionals who work to improve the quality of education for children from birth through age eight. This website contains information about the organization, information for parents and professionals (such as a list of accredited early education programs), public policy issues and news that affects young children, membership information, information on their annual conference, a catalog of resources, and information about NAEYC's accreditation program.

National Association of Child Advocates. http://www.childadvocacy.org

This is a national organization devoted to the creation of state and community based child advocacy organizations. The NACA is active in 44 states and 11 cities and is funded primarily by private foundations and organizations. This website contains information about membership, current projects, links to other sites, publications, and the basics on how to be a child advocate. To contact NACA write to:

National Association of Child Advocates
1522 K Street
Suite 600

Washington, D.C. 20005-1202
Tel: (202) 289-0777
Fax: (202) 289-0776
E-Mail: naca@childadvocacy.org

National Association of Counsel for Children. http://www.naccchildlaw.org
This is a non-profit organization made up of professionals dedicated to the protection of children in the legal system. The NACC provides training and education to attorneys and child advocates and advocates for improved public policy and legislation for children. This website contains information about membership, conferences and training seminars, policy agendas, their quarterly publication (The Guardian), links to other sites, and information about the organization. To contact the NACC write to:
National Association of Counsel for Children
1825 Marion Street
Suite 340
Denver, CO 80218
Tel: (888) 828-NACC
E-Mail: advocate@NACCchildlaw.org

National Association of Early Childhood Teacher Educators. http://www.naecte.org
This membership organization works to promote professional growth and advocates for improvements in early childhood teacher education. This website contains membership information, the NAECTE journal, awards, conferences, links to related organizations, and a list of regional representatives.

National Association of Social Workers. http://www.naswdc.org
This is the largest member organization of professional social workers in the world and works to enhance the professional growth and development of it's members and to advance sound social policies. This site contains information for professional social workers such as continuing education information, a legislative alert section, information on advocacy, and a social work archives containing articles and abstracts from social work journals. There are also sub sections dealing specifically with school social work which address topics such as youth violence and mental health in schools. To contact:

National Association of Social Workers
750 First St. NE, Suite 700
Washington, D.C. 20002-4241
Tel: (202) 408-8600
(800) 638-8799

National Child Care Association. http://www.nccanet.org

This is a professional trade association that focuses on the needs of licensed, private childhood care and education programs. This website contains an issue alert, information on how to join, a list of member state associations, professional development opportunities, federal legislative updates, and for parents lists of who to contact to find out about quality child care in your area. To contact:
National Child Care Association
1016 Rosser St.
Conyers, GA 30012
Tel: (800) 543-7161

National Council of Jewish Women, Inc. http://www.ncjw.org

This is a volunteer organization inspired by Jewish values that works to improve the quality of life for women, children and families through research, education, and advocacy. This site includes current child welfare projects that the council is involved with in both Israel and the United States such as HIPPY, the Home Instruction Program for Pre School Youngsters. To contact:
National Council of Jewish Women
53 West 23rd Street
New York, NY 10010
Tel: (212) 645-4048
Fax: (212) 645-7466

National Council on Family Relations. http://www.ncfr.com

This is a multidisciplinary, nonpartisan organization of educators, researchers, and practitioners who work within family fields. This website contains information about the organization, membership information, on-line journals (**The Journal of Marriage and Family** and **Family Relations**), certification information, family policy, media awards, and information about their annual conference. To contact:

National Council on Family Relations
3989 Central Ave., NE
Suite 550
Minneapolis, MN 55421
Tel: (888) 781-9331
Fax: (612) 781-9348

National Education Association. http://www.nea.org
This membership organization has more than 2.2 million members including teachers, support personnel, retired educators, and students preparing to become teachers. This site contains a wealth of information about education, teaching, students, and schools. There is also a special section for parents, information about the organization, current news and issues in education, legislative action, a press center, publications, information about school safety, grants, and much more. To contact:
National Education Association
1201 16th Street, NW
Washington, DC 20036
Tel: (202) 833-4000

National League for Nursing. http://nln.org
This is an organization representing many of the state visiting nurse associations and home and community health services. This website contains information about the organization, links to state leagues, testing products information, information on the educational summit, continuing education, publications, membership information, on-line journals, an opportunity to search the site for specific information, and employment opportunities. To contact:
National League for Nursing
61 Broadway
New York, NY 10006
Tel: (800) 669-9656
Fax: (607) 723-8408

National School-Age Care Alliance. http://www.nsaca.org
This is a membership organization made up individuals and groups who provide school-age child care. This site contains information about the

organization, current projects and issues, information about professional development and some benefits to being a part of NSACA. Additionally, they provide information about their accreditation to out of school programs and provide a national list of programs which they have accredited. To contact:
National School-Age Alliance
1137 Washington St.
Boston, MA 012142
Tel: (617) 298-5022
Email: staff@nsaca.org

National School Boards Association. http://www.nsba.org
This is a national membership organization whose mission is the advancement of public education. This website contains information about the organization and membership this includes several councils of the National School Boards Association such as the Council of Urban Board Education, Council of School Attorneys, ITTE the Education Technology Programs Department, the Resource Exchange Network, and the National Education Policy Network. Also included is a NSBA library that members and the general public can obtain information from. In the Advocacy section includes information about current NSBA issues such as funding or bilingual education as well as the Legislation Action Center where one can lobby congress via computer. There is also detailed information about the NSBA federation, and a list of education links. To contact:
National School Boards Association
1680 Duke St.
Alexandria, VA 22314
Tel: (7-3) 838-6722
Fax: (703) 683-7590

National Sheriffs' Association. http://www.sheriff.org
This is a private, non-profit professional organization comprised of law enforcement personnel and provides professional training, networking, and information sharing. This website contains information about the organization, congressional affairs, a list of chaplains, publications, information about jail operations, crime prevention, and insurance, research and development, and traffic safety. To contact:
National Sheriffs' Association
1450 Duke St.

Alexandria, VA 22314-3490
Tel: (703) 836-7827

National Youth Employment Coalition. http://www.nyec.org
This is a national network of 150 youth employment and development organizations that provides information and advocacy services in order to increase employment, training opportunities, and education for disadvantaged youth. This website contains information about membership, current issues, reports, legislative information, a calendar of events, and links to other sites. It also includes PEPNet (Promising and Effective Practices Network) which establishes criteria for effectiveness among programs and recognizes excellence in youth programs.

Professional Association for Childhood Education. http://www.pacenet.org
This non-profit membership organization is based in California and works to advance the profession of providing quality child care and early childhood education. It is affiliated with the National Child Care Association. This website contains information about the organization, educational opportunities, publications, information about programs and services, a legislative bill summary list, and membership information.

The Southern Early Childhood Association. http://www.seca50.org
This is a national organization made up of preschool, kindergarten, and primary teachers and administrators, caregivers, programs directors, and individuals working with and for families to promote quality care and education for young children, with a particular commitment to southern issues. This website contains information about SECA and how to join, their annual conference, publications and resources which include: books, videos and professional development institutes that members and non members can order. The site also includes a list of their affiliated state chapters, and information updates. To contact:
Southern Early Childhood Association
7107 W. 12th, Suite 102
Little Rock, AK 72215-5930
Tel: (800) 305-7322
Fax: (501) 63302114
E-Mail: seca@aristotle.net

Stand For Children. http://www.stand.org

This is a membership organization affiliated with the Children's Defense Fund that works to find local solutions to children's issues of health, safety, and education. This website contains information about the organization, highlights from different state chapters, membership information, a book store through amazon.com, child care and organizing resources, current and past issues of *Stand Up* newsletter, and an opportunity to take action by emailing congress. It also includes "issue areas" about health care, child care, education, violence and out of school programs. To contact Stand for Children:

Stand for Children
1834 Connecticut Ave., NW
Washington, DC 20009
Tel: (800) 663-4032
(202) 234-0095
Fax: (202) 234-0217
E-Mail: tellstand@stand.org

World Association for Infant Mental Health. http://www.msu.edu/user/waimh/left.htm

This is an international and interdisciplinary association that promotes scientific and clinical studies of infants, their caregivers, and the caregiving context. This website is sponsored by Michigan State University and contains information about the organization, a member list, a Infant Mental Health Journal, an on-line journal, a call for papers, publications, videos, professional information about infant mental health training, and links to other sites.

Chapter 19

CONCLUSIONS

There are thousands of locations that exist which have information about children. More will develop over time. This means that the amount of time necessary to conduct a comprehensive investigation on any child related topic will increase. It also means that the degree of sophistication of the investigator must also improve. As more and more information becomes obtainable through the electronic medium, it is possible that child well being could be improved because more of the data researchers need is easily available.

However, having more information does not necessarily mean that better information will be used. It is essential that electronic researchers develop a keen eye and understanding of what constitutes good quality information, and what does not. There is much poor quality information available. For the sake of the children, it is important to know the difference.

Remember, research is an art, and not everyone is cut out to be an artist. If this type of investigation is too tedious or frustrating, there are a variety of consultants who are expert in this area with whom you can contract to help you find what you need.

But everyone who is willing should now be able to find information on children's issues. We hope that by compiling information that previously was difficult to locate that your task will become easier, and your outcomes more successful.

INDEX

A

About Face, 121
Abstinence Education Program, 36
Action Alliance for Children, 45
Ad Council, 121
Administration for Children and Families, 28, 31, 32, 34, 118, 151, 156
Administration on Children, Youth and Families, 32, 33, 34, 118, 151, 156
Adolescent Directory On-Line, 135
adoption packet, 116
adoption statistics, 118, 156
Advocates for Youth, 135
African American Resources, 136
after school programs, 30, 66, 73
after-school recreation, 4
Agency for Health Care Policy and Research, 34, 151
Alliance for Children and Families, 171
Alpha Center, 87
America Links Up, 136
American Academy of Adoption Attorneys, 171
American Academy of Child and Adolescent Psychiatry, 172
American Academy of Pediatrics, 80, 87, 88, 172
American Association for Marriage and Family Therapy, 173
American Association of Family and Consumer Services, 173
American Association of School Administrators, 87, 173, 174
American Association on Mental Retardation, 174
American Bar Association Center on Children and the Law, 59, 174
American Camping Association, 14, 127
American Civil Liberties Union, 46
American Coalition for Abuse Awareness Newsletter, 101
American College of Nurse-Midwives, 175
American Counseling Association, 175
American Health Foundation, 88
American Humane Association, 151, 152
American Indian Research and Policy Institute, 46, 151
American Library Association, 77
American Medical Association, 88, 176
American Nurses Association, 176

American Professional Society on the Abuse of Children, 102, 176
American Psychoanalytic Association, 176, 177
American Psychological Association, 177
American Public Health Association, 89, 177
American Public Human Services Association, 178
American Red Cross, 137
American School Counselor Association, 178
American Youth Policy Forum, 47
Annie E. Casey Foundation, 164
Aspen Publishers, Inc, 163
Aspiring Youth, 78
Association for Children for Enforcement of Support, 60
Association of America's Public Television Stations, 122
Association of Jewish Sponsored Camps, 128
Association of Teacher Educators, 178

B

battered child syndrome, 20
Benton Foundation, 51, 164
Best Fed, 51, 89, 164
Better Business Bureau, 123
birth defects information, 97, 156
body image project, 81
Boolean operators, 18, 19
Boy Scouts of America, 128
Boys Town National Research Hospital, 89, 128
Bureau of Justice Statistics, 39, 40, 152
Bureau of Labor Statistics, 40, 152
Bureau of Transportation Statistics, 41, 153

C

California Community Foundation, 164

California Early Childhood Mentor Program, 65
Campaign for Our Children, 137, 153
CareGuide, 66
Carnegie Corporation, 90, 165
Carnegie Foundation, 165
Casey Family Program, 113
Catholic Charities, 131
Center for Career Development in Early Childhood Education, 78
Center for Child and Family Policy, 47
Center for Disease Control and Prevention, 34, 47, 97, 153, 158
Center for Health Care Strategies, 90, 97, 158
Center for Law and Social Policy, 60, 90
Center for Media Education, 122
Center for Media Literacy, 122
Center for Mental Health Services, 38, 153
Center for the Child Care Workforce, 66
Center for the Improvement of Child Caring, 66
Center on Budget and Policy Priorities, 47, 48
Centers for Disease Control and Prevention (CDC), 31, 34
Chapin Hall Center for Children, 48
Charles Stewart Mott Foundation, 165
charter schools, 26, 30
child abuse, 7, 16, 18, 20, 26, 29, 31, 33, 34, 49, 57, 59, 99, 101, 102, 103, 104, 105, 106, 107, 108, 109, 110, 116, 117, 133, 148, 150, 153, 154, 155, 174, 179
Child Abuse Prevention Network, 102, 153
child abuse research, 102, 154
child advocacy, 1, 9, 49, 132, 148, 180
Child and Family News, 138
child bereavement, 133
Child Care Action Campaign, 67
Child Care Aware, 67
Child Care Bureau, 32, 34
child care expenses, 67
Child Care Experts National Network, 67

Index

Child Care Law Center, 61, 67, 68
child care provider, 69
child development, 29, 30, 33, 56, 61, 68, 140, 144, 150
child health, 1, 26, 33, 34, 36, 38, 42, 87, 88, 92, 94, 95, 98, 99, 152, 166, 172, 177
Child Protection Clearinghouse, 102
Child Rights Information Network, 48
Child Safety, viii, ix, 101, 103
child support enforcement, 28, 31, 59, 60, 160
Child Support Information Site, 114
Child Trends, Inc, 49
Child Victims Act Model Courts Project, 119
Child Welfare Institute, 138
Child Welfare League of America, 50, 144
Child Welfare Research, 49, 50
Children and Family Research Center, 114, 138
Children and Violence- Prevention Program, 103
Children Awaiting Parents, 114, 116
Children Now, 50, 51, 123
Children of Alcoholics Foundation, 139
Children of Separation and Divorce Center, 114, 115
children with special needs, 32, 100, 142
Children, Youth and Family Consortium, 115, 139
Children's Defense Fund, 3, 15, 140, 154, 186
Children's Environmental Health Network, 90
Children's Foundation, 141
Children's Health Indicators, 91, 154
Children's Health Insurance Program, 56, 91, 100, 161
Children's Health Protection, 41
Children's Institute International, 103
children's law manual, 62
Children's Legal Right's Journal, 62
Children's Music Web, 78

Children's Partnership, 123
Children's Rights Council, 115
Children's Safety Network, 104
Children's Television Workshop, 123
civil rights, 39, 136
class size, 30
Coalition for America's Children, 51
Coalition for Asian-American Children and Families, 141, 155
Colorado Children's Campaign, 141
Comer School Development Program, 79
Committee for Economic Development, 51
Common Core of Data (CCD), 31
Commonwealth Fund, 91, 166
communication programs, 4
community building, 48, 56
Concept-based searching, 17
Congregations Concerned for Children, 132
Corporation for Public Broadcasting, 124
Council for Exceptional Children, 142, 179
Council for Professional Recognition, 68
Council of the Great City Schools, 79
counseling services, 4, 114, 133
credit history, 70
crib laws, 166
Crime and Justice Data Abstracts, 39, 152
cyber rights, 46

D

Danny Foundation, 166
David and Lucille Packard Foundation, 166
Day Care Providers, 68
death penalty, 46, 61
Developing Educational Standards, 79
disability rights, 46
disease outbreak news, 100
Doll Project, 141
drug policy, 46
drug rehabilitation centers, 133

E

Early Childhood Education Linkage System, 80
Ed Source, 80
educational alternatives, 4
Educational Resources Information Center (ERIC), 77, 80
Electronic Activist, 41
Electronic Policy Network, 52
employer based health programs, 97
environmental health, 87, 88, 90
ERIC data base, 30
Even Start Family Literacy Program, 81
Expedited Adoptions project, 119

F

Faces of Adoption, 114, 116
faith based organizations, 57
Families and Work Institute, 116, 117
Families and Youth Services Bureau, 33
Families Report on Children's Well Being, 8
family loan program, 57
Family Preservation and Child Welfare Network, 116, 155
Family Resource Coalition of America, 116
Family Resource Information, Education, & Network Development Services, 104
family violence, 116, 133, 155
federal advocacy, 98
Federal Communications Commission, 28
federal day care centers, 67
Federal Web Locator, 42
Fedstats, 25, 42, 151, 155
financial aid information, 30, 160
financial assistance, 31, 32, 67
Focus Adolescent Services, 142
food assistance, 48, 93
Food Research and Action Center, 93
Ford Foundation, 166, 167

foster care, 26, 27, 33, 42, 49, 59, 63, 113, 116, 117, 120, 149, 155, 174
Foster Care Connections, 113, 117
Foster Children United, 120
Foster Parent Pages, 117
Foundation Center, 163, 167, 169
4-H programs, 30
Frank Stanley Beveridge Foundation, 167
free speech, 46
fresh air camps, 133
Future of Children Journal, 166

G

gay and lesbian rights, 46
gender inequality, 35
Girl Power, 35
Girl Scouts of the USA, 128
Girls, Inc., 124
Global ChildNet, 94
Global Health Network, 94
Gun Violence, 105, 143

H

HANDSNet, 143
Harvard Center for Children's Health, 94
Head Start, 31, 32, 33, 34, 54, 68, 69, 83, 151
Health Care Financing Administration, 35, 91, 95, 155
health care policies, 5
health care programs, 35, 95, 155
Health Resources and Services Administration (HRSA), 36
Healthy Childcare, 69
Hearst Foundation, 167
HIV policy, 96, 168
Hofstra Law Review, 126
Human Rights USA, 143

I

I Am Your Child Campaign, 143

Index

Idea Central, 52
immunodeficiency disorders, 96
infant disease, 36
infant health statistics, 97, 156
Infant Mental Health, 186
infant mortality, 36, 97, 156
Information Clearinghouse on Children, 53
Injury Control Resource Information Network, 101, 105, 156
injury specific resources, 105, 156
Institute for Child Health Policy, 87, 95
Institute for Research on Poverty, 53
Insure Kids Now, 35, 93
Interfaith Alliance, 132
International Nanny Association, 69
International Society for the Prevention of Child Abuse and Neglect, 105, 179
Internet Nonprofit Center, 144
Internet Online Summit, 144

J

Jewish Board of Family and Children's Services, 132
job openings, 56
Journal of Early Intervention, 142
Just Think Foundation, 81
Juvenile Justice Center, 61
Juvenile Justice Clearinghouse, 59, 62

K

Kaiser Family Foundation, 96, 168
Kidd Safety, 29
Kids Care, 96
Kids Growth, 144
KidsHealth, 88, 96, 176
KidsNet, 124
Kidsource Online, 96
KidsPeace, 144
KinderCam, 70

L

learning styles, 178
lessonplan data base, 81
Library of Congress, v, 28
library web resources, 77
listserv links, 57
low income housing, 48
low-income children, 33, 56, 60, 90

M

malnutrition, 93
March of Dimes, 97, 156
McKnight Foundation, 57, 168
Media Forum, 124
Media Literacy On-line Project, 125
Media Research Center, 125
Mediascope, 125
Medicaid, 5, 31, 35, 90, 91, 92, 95, 96, 97, 131, 155, 166, 168
Medicare, 35, 95, 155
MedWeb, 97
Member and Committee Information of Congress, 26
Merrow Report, 81
Military Child Development Program, 29
Minnesota Center Against Violence and Abuse, 106
missing children alerts, 109
Montessori in the Home, 81
Morrison Institute for Public Policy, 54
motor vehicle reports, 70
multicultural education, 178
multimedia classroom, 81
music education, 78

N

nanny agencies, 70
National 4-H, 128
National Adoption Information Clearinghouse, 113, 118, 156
National Alliance for the Mentally Ill, 180

National Association for Family Child Care, 71
National Association for the Education of Young Children, 82, 180
National Association of Child Advocates, 180
National Association of Child Care Resource and Referral Agencies, 70
National Association of Counsel for Children, 62, 181
National Association of Early Childhood Teacher Educators, 181
National Association of Safe Schools, 77, 82
National Association of Social Workers, 181, 182
National Black Child Development Institute, 145
National Camp Association, 129
National Center for Children in Poverty, 54, 56, 157
National Center for Education Statistics, 31, 100, 155, 157, 160, 161
National Center for Health Statistics, 34, 97, 158
National Center for Missing and Exploited Children, 145
National Center for Youth Law, 63
National Center on Child Fatality Review, 107
national child abuse hotline, 102, 154
National Child Care Association, 71, 182, 185
National Child Care Information Center, 32, 65, 71, 72
National Child Rights Alliance, 106
National Children's Advocacy Center, 107
National Clearinghouse for Alcohol and Drug Information, 145
National Clearinghouse on Child Abuse, 101, 104, 107
National Coalition for the Homeless, 7, 146

National Committee on Vital and Health Statistics, 36, 158
National Committee to Prevent Child Abuse, 108, 110
National Conference of State Legislatures, 26
National Council of Jewish Women, Inc, 182
National Council on Family Relations, 182, 183
National Court Appointed Special Advocate Association, 63
National Crime Prevention Council, 108
National Data Archive on Child Abuse and Neglect, 102, 108, 154
National Directory of Children, Youth and Family Services, 146
National Early Childhood Technical Assistance System, 146
National Education Association, 183
National Educational Service, 82
National Family Preservation Network, 118
National Foundation for Abused and Neglected Children, 109
National Governors' Association, 27
National Health Law Program News, 97
National Indian Child Welfare Association, 147
National Institute on Early Childhood Development and Education, 83
National Institute on Out-Of-School Time, 72
National Institutes of Health (NIH), 31
National League for Nursing, 183
National Library of Medicine, 98
National Longitudinal Study of Adolescent Health, 98, 159
National Network for Child Care, 72
National Network for Youth, 55
National Parent Information Network, 147
National Parenting Association, 147, 148
National Partnership for Women and Families, 55

Index

National PTA, 83
National Resource Center for Health and Safety in Child Care, 73
National Resource Center for Youth Services, 148
National Resource Center on Child Maltreatment, 109, 138
National School Boards Association, 184
National School-Age Care Alliance, 73, 183
national security, 46
National Sheriffs' Association, 184
National Society for the Prevention of Cruelty to Children, 109
National Youth Employment Coalition, 185
Neglect Data System, 33
non-custodial parents, 57
Nonprofit Gateway, 42
non-profit organization, 46, 50, 55, 56, 57, 60, 62, 66, 68, 70, 74, 78, 82, 83, 84, 85, 90, 92, 93, 96, 97, 100, 102, 103, 109, 113, 114, 115, 116, 119, 120, 121, 122, 125, 129, 132, 135, 137, 139, 141, 142, 144, 145, 147, 150, 152, 155, 171, 178, 181
nonprofit organizations, 42
not-for-profit organizations, 5

O

Occupational Safety and Health Administration, 40, 159
Office of Disease Prevention and Health Promotion, 37, 98
Office of Genetics and Disease Prevention, 34
Office of Health Policy, 38, 99
online periodicals, 77
on-line press kit, 142

P

PACER Center, 84

parent education, 4, 66
Parents Guide to the Information Superhighway, 123
Parents Television Council, 125
Partnership Against Violence, 43, 109
Pathways to School Improvement, 84
Pediatric Points of Interest, 99
pediatric services, 89
pediatric surgical conditions, 100
peer support networks, 4
Permanency Planning for Children, 119
Physical Activity and Health, 99
preschools, 66
Prevent Child Abuse America, 110, 117
Prevention Yellow Pages, 148
probation homes, 133
Problem Solver, 84
Professional Association for Childhood Education, 185
Project for the Future of Equal Justice, 60
public assistance, 32, 57
Public Broadcasting Service, 126
Pueblo Child Advocacy Center, 148

R

racial and cultural issues, 98
Rare Genetic Diseases In Children, 99
recall information, 29
reproductive health, 96, 98, 168
reproductive rights, 46
Research and Training Center in Rehabilitation and Childhood Trauma, 110
Research Forum on Children, Families, and the New Federation, 56
Robert Wood Johnson Foundation, 168
Rockefeller Foundation, 79
Route 6-16, 148

S

Safe Kids, 40, 110
safe nursery products, 166